Words Walk is a selection of word poems, short stories, and personal essays. Words are employed to capture the essence, spirit, or value of the author's perceptions of the events, situations, and circumstances of his borrowed and earned experiences. The book explores the emotional, the happy, the offbeat, the sad, and the whimsical. Words have the capacity to knot our guts, massage our hearts, bring us to laughter, and exercise our minds. The focus is on the images drawn from both the breadth (the number of words) and the depth (the number of usages per word) of our vocabularies and the impacts such words have on our lives.

—Ronald M. Ruble

WORDS WALK

Ronald M. Ruble (signature)

RONALD M. RUBLE

J.P. —
You are special + I value
our friendship over the years —
you are a great friend!
Best wishes — RM (AKA Gestalt)
6/2013

BIRD DOG PUBLISHING

HURON, OHIO

© 2013 Ronald M. Ruble & Bird Dog Publishing,
An imprint of Bottom Dog Press
ISBN 978-1-933964-71-3
Bottom Dog Press
PO Box 425
Huron, Ohio 44839
http://smithdocs.net
e-mail: Lsmithdog@smithdocs.net

CREDITS:
General Editor: Susanna Sharp-Schwacke
Layout & Design: Susanna Sharp-Schwacke
Cover Design: Susanna Sharp-Schwacke
Cover Photos: Ronald M. Ruble
Author's Photo: Brent Fantozzi

Table of Contents

9-11-1	13
Adjectives	14
Adverbs	15
Albums	16
Ask	17
Aware	18
Baptism	19
Bedlam	21
Bolt	24
Cicadas	25
Circles and Cycles	26
Conjunctions	27
Crack	28
Daughters	29
Dearness of it All	30
Disruption	31
Dongle	33
Down Time	35
Dreams	37
Driven	38
Echoes	40
Essence	42
Exquisite	43
Eyes	44
Fall Rain	45
Flowers	46
Gathering	48
Gerunds	50
Girls in White	51
Green	53
Guernica	56
Gut	57
Handprint	59
Have You Noticed?	60
Highway	62
Hoar Frost	63
Honest Work	64
Hugs	65
I Wonder	67
Iceman	68
If	70
In The Flight of A Feather	71

INFINITIVES	72
KALEIDOSCOPES	74
LEAF RAKER	76
LIFE IS	78
LOGAN'S CREEK	80
LOONS	82
MAGIC	83
MASKS	84
MELTING IMAGES	85
MY FREEZER	86
NERVOUS	93
NIGHT SYMPHONY	94
NIGHT TIME	95
NO CHOICE	96
NOCTURNE	98
NOUNS	99
OLD BARN	100
ORNATE	101
OVER	102
PAS DE DEUX	104
PAST PARTICIPLES	105
PATH	106
PONDERABLES	108
PREPOSITIONS	110
QUANDARY	112
QUESTIONS	113
QUICK	114
QUIT	116
RANCID	118
REBUKE	120
REMINDERS	121
RESPLENDENT TAPESTRY	122
ROADS	123
RUMINATE	125
RUSTLINGS	126
SEASONAL DEBRIS	127
SHATTERED WINDSHIELD	128
SHOES	130
SO MANY TIMES	131
SOLITARY	133
SONS	134
SPECIAL PEOPLE	135
SYCAMORE	136
TEARS	137
TENDER TIMES	138

THEN AGAIN	140
THIS CHURCH	141
THE TIME IS NOW	143
TIME WAS	144
TRACKS	145
UBIQUITOUS	146
ULTIMATE	147
UNKNOWN	148
USAGES	149
USELESS	150
VERBS	151
VERTIGO	153
WATERING HOLE	154
WHEN ALL IS SAID AND DONE	155
WHY	156
WIN OR LOSE	157
WINTER CREAKS	158
WISDOM	159
WITHIN THE SUBLIME	160
WORDS WALK	161
YAP	162
ABOUT THE AUTHOR	163

Dedication

To the Rubles: Eric, Amanda, Lauryn; Kris, Jen, Corrinne, Kirstyn, Hunter, Parker, and Kayelyn.

To my parents Al and Dessie Briner, my Ruble sisters Jackie Lou and Janice, my brother Bud Briner and his wife Janet.

"Words walk. They take us by the hand and escort us to places where our minds and imaginations thrive."
—Ronald M. Ruble

"The words of a man's mouth are deep waters; the wellspring of wisdom is a flowing brook"
Proverbs 18:4

"Some use cameras and film, others paint or charcoal, many the musical scale or movement, still others employ metals, woods, clay, or concrete, some use fabrics, yarns and cloth, still others play roles on a stage. I am in the tradition of words."
—Ronald M. Ruble

"Actions speak louder than words, but not nearly as often."
—Mark Twain

9-11-1

Terrorists gave birth to shards.
Pieces of glass, metal, bone…
rained on Manhattan, Washington,
and Pennsylvania, September 11, 2001.
Uncountable numbers of missiles
lacerating comfort, confidence,
contentment and complacency.
Severing utilities; reducing to dust
icons of capitalism;
cracking the foundations of
democracy and freedom;
amputating and pruning limbs from
family trees with forces greater
than hurricanes and tornadoes.
Blood and horror seeped through a
tapestry of red, white, and blue,
cutting open the American
fabric and spirit.
Death pierced the hearts of uncountable
numbers of peaceful people around the world.
Shock and inaction gave way
to duty and action; disbelief then anger
gave way to patriotism then reaction.
Empathy and sympathy asserted themselves;
we gathered and absorbed each others' tears and fears.
The beauty of streaking white contrails
against an azure blue sky
take on a frightening significance now.
We hold hands and chant:
"We will not tolerate blind hates to rain their
shards and fragments;
to molest and rape our land of the free.
We will not tolerate it.
We will not!"

Adjectives

We are taught that adjectives
are words that modify a noun.
Early on, I did not realize
that nouns needed help.
Later, I came to understand that
I could not speak or write without using adjectives
because nouns cannot stand alone.
"Child" does not work, as a word by itself,
because people want to know
if child is good, tall, fat, skinny, quarrelsome,
sensitive, angelic, mean, dirty, precocious,
wicked, nasty, offensive, or contemptible.
We all know what "female," "male," and "worker" mean.
However, value and worth are dependent upon knowing
if the female or male worker is diligent, good, affable,
profane, stubborn, disrespectful, scurrilous, or competent.
Being a "parent" is not enough;
one must be caring, nurturing, virtuous, affectionate, loving,
or devoted to be viewed as an admirable parent.
The nouns "idea" and "notion" appear to be weak,
on their own, until the communicator couples them with
righteous, kinky, lurid, abhorrent, gullible, impulsive, noble,
judicious, empty, repugnant, immoral, or contagious.
Authors focus, in some way, on a "climax" in their work.
Climaxes can be predictable, heart-thumping,
hypnotic, obscure, disappointing, superb, horrifying, and valiant,
or, ecstatic, traumatic, rousing, bountiful, spectacular, orbital,
and explosive depending on the author's story line.
But a climax without the adjective is, shall we say, dull.
In short, our reactions rely on adjectives for maturation of the noun.
Being viewed as a "writer" is important to me.
I am always curious as to whether my writing is perceived as capable,
exciting, humorous, obscure, verbose, tender or flatulent.

Adverbs

He found himself inside
looking out…outward somewhere
he did not recognize.
Before yesterday he never imagined
he would find himself so
recklessly, mindlessly, urgently
running anywhere yet everywhere
blindly racing into and
roughly bouncing off of objects
awkwardly falling down
feverishly climbing slippery slopes
grimly hoping to get away from
the brutally painful spasms
that stressfully twisted inside his chest.
The absurdly horrible thoughts
that drunkenly caromed inside his head.
He instinctively gulped for air
and quickly searched for a way out.
Not quite able to discern better or worse
he hesitantly stood and
most carefully inched his way
toward the breath of air
he felt timidly caressing his cheek;
toward the beam of light
that was to lead him home.

Albums

Our lives are filled
with connected moments,
cradled in the heart.
Some are distant, others new
some are sad, others glad.
We go through life together
reminded of the union
of two to become one.

The loving images mirrored in the
beauty of our offspring's eyes;
a floodtide of our years nourishes our embrace
with each wave of affection that caresses our shore.

Each kiss, laced with the flavor of the giver,
satisfies our palates.
This social snack embosses the stamped seals;
secures the testament between us.

When we reach into each other
we are greeted by moments
of our friends and relatives; our parents,
brothers, sisters,
daughters, sons, grandchildren
and the two of us.

Contentment and understanding connect
our minds with our hearts.
Tears well in our eyes and
cascade down our cheeks.
A private baptism only we,
in this moment of sharing,
can translate fully.

We have been blessed.
Our esteemed albums filled with
the moments of our lives, are bursting!
We are balanced, in harmony, centered.

We pledge to hold these albums dear.
They are unique; our bond.

Ask

Flesh, all black and charred,
    echo eyes that appear barred.
Cartilage and ligaments torn,
    looking like he had never been born.

Guts all gnarled and twisted in knots,
    trying to spew forth from large red dots.
Surprise, shock, and disbelief
    etched onto his face ever so brief.

Anger, hate, pity, and fear
    all scream out for us to hear.
Death affects both body and soul,
    all for the sake of playing a role.

I feel sick and full of guilt,
    man tears down what God has built.
All around us men lay dying;
    no one is left to do the crying.

Like bees swarming a honey tree,
    maggots infest my friend and me.
Death often comes in different ways
    but in the heart it really stays.

Death can be slow or fast,
    but it is sorrow that makes it last.
The tear on his cheek runs a straight line!
    Oh, dear God! Is it his...or mine?

"Have you ever killed a man?"

"Ask me something...white...."

Aware

My heart swells, breathing halts,
eyes mist over, head spins a bit.
Does he know he has the audience
in the palms of his hands?
Does he feel that magic?

Children sit on the edge of their seats;
adults watch him intently
as he moves about the stage.
He commands the moment!
The hairs on my body rise to attention
as my excitement and pleasure build.
He is comfortable in the spotlight.
He commands my focus!
Does he know how natural he is?

He ambles about,
hunched over and squat-like at the knees.
His graveled voice rises and falls
in a storyteller's lilt.
He peers at me through and over
wire-rimmed glasses.
His smile charms me, warms my heart.
His hands, dynamic and marvelous,
orchestrate the action,
moment by moment, scene by scene.
He manipulates me; I am his puppet.
Is he aware of his power over me?

At the age of fourteen,
he masters a character
five decades older than he.
When I was fourteen,
I dreamed of being able to do that.
Does he know how good he is?
Does he know his acting potential?
Is he aware of the pride I have in him?

Baptism

Snowflakes flutter down, fragile and soft
    as chaff seeping through cracks in an old hayloft.
Miniature works of art, tiny doilies of lace
    swirl toward the ground as if each has a place.

They caress the soil and their beauty shines through,
    then they melt and disappear right in front of you.
Each flake bombards your face like pricks from a pin,
    their life span is short moisturizing your skin.

Stand in the driveway until you become wet,
    an experience of nature you will never forget.
Frosted cobwebs streaking down from above
    one of many ways that nature sends love.

"A word is dead when it's been said, some say. I say it just begins to live that day."

—Emily Dickinson

Bedlam

There's a gaping incision
    in the wholeness of parenthood,
which occurs when our children exert their independency
    to go out on their own.

Our responses to such departures,
    in the immediacy of the moment,
    may be to celebrate.
To congratulate ourselves on a job well done;
    to breathe a sigh of relief
    that we've honored the age old tradition
    of supplying the next generation.
A generation we pledge to be better than our own.

We greet the product of our loins
    with tears of joy and relief
    spattering upon antiseptic, starched linens.
That first cry reverberates off the germ-free tiles
    and sets us adrift on a crazy,
    dizzying journey into the wilderness of parenthood.

Throughout this voyage we often struggle over
    how to push aside "me," an entity we've been devoted to;
    a part so integral to our unity
    that we alter states for;
    we modify our needs, wants, desires
    tastes, priorities, and securities for.
So now we work to incorporate "we" into this part of our identity;
    a task often filled with trial and error.

These children we've nurtured, directed, protected, watched over,
    been worried about, couldn't sleep because of,
    cried over and cried with, wiped tears from,
    nursed when ill, bandaged cuts and scrapes for,
    comforted and played with when lonely,
    rocked to sleep, and covered to keep the chill out.
Reprimanded and scolded when necessary,
    provided a safe haven when frightened,
    taught right from wrong,
    instilled a faith and morality, the Golden Rule,
    honesty, integrity, and hugged and kissed
    without conditions.

Our children,
> who walk into tomorrow and stand
> shoulder to shoulder with other children.

Those with arrogance,
> who smack out at parents with the terse coda,
> "You had to do those things.
> It was your obligation. I didn't ask to be born."

Those same children,
> who on national television,
> at the ages of eleven and twelve,
> shout defiantly into the faces of their parents,
> "It's my body. I can do what I want.
> If I've got it, why not flaunt it?"

Those same children,
> whose eyes lack sparkle,
> and whose smiles seem unnatural
> as if too infrequently displayed, and
> who at the ages of fourteen and fifteen
> command their parents to,
> "Shut up. Get a life. Get the hell out of mine!"

Those same children who honor their threats
> by joining those already homeless on the streets,
> those who kill other children, rob and beat the defenseless,
> those who dumpster dive, pander and prostitute,
> and those whose addictions lead them to
> final resting places well before their times;
> in condemned tenement houses, warehouses,
> deserted subways, dense forest thickets,
> rusty junkyards, mud-thickened slimy rivers, and
> in cardboard boxes in darkened back alleys that cops won't
> even bother to enter…places void of love or care.

Respect my need for heritage…
> one with grandchildren and great-grandchildren.

Try to be tolerant of my fears
> and outcries over such bedlam.

For these are matters of import.

I am before you in all my male nakedness,
> sounding suspiciously stereotypical.

But love and caring have no gender.

Allow me to clutch the photo albums
    which house the frozen moments
    in time of my sons....

Indulge me, because I am convinced
    they will never be as safe again.

Bolt

I wonder at the variety of uses this four letter word has.
According to *Webster's New Dictionary and
Thesaurus*, bolt, as a noun, can convey "bar, bound,
catch, dart, dash, escape, fastener, flight, flit, latch,
lock, missile, peg, pin, projectile, shaft, sprint, and
thunderbolt" to list a few.

Ah, but we aren't done yet. Bolt, used as a verb can
suggest "abscond, devour, discharge, elope, expel,
fasten, flee, gobble, gorge, gulp, guzzle, sprint,
stuff, and wolf" and then some.

As an overeater, insecure being,
and from time to time a flight freak,
I am the embodiment of bolt.

Cicadas

Hear my presence
    high in the Catalpas;
enticing you, connecting to your youth,
    reach to me;
ride the shifting breeze
    high to my perch.
Sing with me as the sun
    warms our hearts.
Cradled gently among
    the bean pods;
get here before the
    winged death that
    prey upon me do.
I've waited so long to meet
    with you again, and
    am gone oh so soon.
I leave behind my shell as
    a remembrance of our
    too short embrace.
Dread not, weep not; I will return and
    we will sing together again.

RONALD M. RUBLE

CIRCLES AND CYCLES

Circular and spiral arrangements which
measure the courses of time and distance everywhere.
They are orbits, rings, ages,
poems, plays, novels, and songs.
They are intervals of time;
seconds, minutes, hours, days, weeks,
months, years, decades, centuries.
At times they are wheels of
one, two, three, four; or
cylinders of two, four, six or eight.
Dogs circle to lie down.
Liquids circle drains
clockwise here;
counterclockwise there.
A circle could be a series of events
leading back to a starting point,
if you get the point,
or know where it is.
We learn to sing their lyrics
and dance their beats as children;
to study their history as students;
to endure their vibrations and oscillations as adults.
Sometimes we whirl about as
centrifugal force tries to
drive us from the merry-go-round
while the cylinder spins
faster and faster;
we feel lightheaded
and gurgle forth laughter.
Other times, we hang on for dear life
as centripetal force
threatens to suck us inward,
closer to the bottomless black hole;
the noise isn't of our laughter
but of the gasps and screams of
of the frustrated, angered, and afraid.
Round and round they go;
stepping stones in the cycle of life.

Conjunctions

Joiners are they;
    necessary to bring
        words, phrases, or clauses
            together in harmony.

Cucumbers and sandwiches;
    pimples and cream;
        difficult yet attainable;
            innocent yet guilty.

Neither raisins nor nuts;
    neither here nor there;
        for he so loved her;
            for she was so pretty.

Or challenge but not deny;
    or accept but not begrudge.

Where would one be if not
    for joiners?

Crack

His body was twisted, pretzel like,
as if he died in pain and agony.
Not like someone who expired
with peace, on his back,
hands at his sides.
His claw-like hands suggested an effort
to undo what was already done.

Tootsie Pop...the street name for a sixteen
year old kid who became a candy man in seventh grade.
His habit cleaved him in two, top to bottom; the half you got
depended on whether he was up or down, Tootsie or Popped.

The report of his death will permeate every nook and cranny
of this decaying neighborhood.
Desperate people will crash into one another,
unfocused, in their rush to find another candy man.
It never seemed to hit home to Freddy
that his candy was like a loaded revolver
with a hair trigger.

I pull my raincoat up and over his head.
I hope that will erase the bug-eyed
distortion frozen on his face.
I close my eyes and pull out the drawer
in the history file of my mind;
open the folder to look at the beautiful twelve year old
with sparkling eyes, wide smile, and raised eyebrows.
A face filled with excitement, innocence and hope.
A captured moment frozen in time;
a time before the spiral to the end.

That's the Freddie I want to remember.
I never knew Tootsie Pop.

Daughters

My sons brought me my daughters.
My daughters brought a refreshing change
into my household and thinking.
Having fathered no daughters, I had
forgotten much of the growing up years
of my life with two sisters sharing the house.
My new daughters reminded me
of my need to reorient!

Their perspective is femininity;
their scent, taste, and touch add to
the depth and texture of my palate.
Whereas my sons tend to see the
beauty of the whole forest with the
eagle and crow flying above it,
as do I perhaps,
my daughters see the trees,
their changing leaves, hear the
sounds of the squirrels and chipmunks,
and smell the fragrance of the forest flowers.
They have brought curtains,
a sense of decor, and style into my life.

The Dearness of it All

Is there anything more dear to parents
than their children?
Sprigs on the family tree
are to be cherished and nourished
because they are destined
to produce the next fruit.
If you will allow them, they will
play hide-and-seek in your heart.
Their giggles call you in;
once there, you can dance hand in hand
with the sparkling imp within.
The looks in their eyes
usher you in on their terms.
Darling and lovable, these offspring
remind us of the sweetness of honey,
to be tasted again and again.
Then come the children of your children;
the cycle begins again.
You love on a level not experienced
before, one that beckons,
takes you to new places,
fills you with energy and an endearing
song that never leaves your mind.
Spritely in tempo, soothing in tone,
nourishing in harmony,
strong in its beat,
the music massages your heart
and coaxes a smile
even on your darkest days.

Disruption

At the phone's ring,
muscles surge,
skin tightens,
hairs raise up,
pulling you out of your dream.
Three in the morning.
No one calls at this time of night.
Slowly you push covers back,
edge toward the phone,
not sure you want to pick it up.
Your pores tingle trying to
decide if they should release moisture.
The loud ring cuts through the darkness again,
pierces into your stomach,
warning you of impending danger.
You hold the phone;
it rings again.
You almost drop it as
sweat begins to seep.
"Hello," you answer.
Nothing but silence and the sound
of your heart pounding.
Then the voice,
"Is Harry there? I need to talk to Harry."
Music and laughter reverberate
in the background.
"Harry, is that you?"
"Harry doesn't live here," you reply.
"Where does he live?"
"I don't know," you reply.
"He gave me this phone number."
"Then he gave you the wrong one," you reply.
"Well, when you find Harry,
tell him Spencer called."
Click. Silence.

RONALD M. RUBLE

You put the phone down,
crawl back into bed,
eyes wide open you wonder
Who is Harry?
Where does he live?
And who the hell is Spencer?
The more you try to erase the questions,
the longer your eyes remain open.
Sleep does not return.

Dongle

"So, how's your dongle?"
In the moment before my response
I wondered, person, place, or thing?
"Just fine and yours?"
I replied without knowing
what a dongle was.

"Why it's a person!"
Gunther and Barbra Dongle
exclaimed someone in the crowd
with Gestalt Dongle echoing their cry.
"A wonderful place," sighs Dingledine,
harbor master of Dongle Island,
as he leans back against the mast of his
sail boat, the "Darling Dongle."

"To dongle, or not to dongle,"
might be a Shakespearean inquiry.
Einstein might have stated,
"A dongle is a double D minus squared."
Sophocles might have shared,
"With a dongle comes great wisdom."
Orwell might have contended that,
"A dongle is doublespeak."
Camus might have asserted,
"To dongle is to be not free."
While Pirandello might have surmised,
"It is, if you think it is."

My friend JP said, "You can't
get along without a dongle.
A dongle is essential to dongle
or to go dongling."

I began to think that everyone
had a dongle; why not me?
If a dongle is a must have,
why don't I have a dongle?

RONALD M. RUBLE

        I immediately Googled "dongle"
       to joyfully discover that I have one.
        I now look at my dongle with
       renewed respect and admiration.

Down Time

Down time is doing nothing
except the bare minimum.

A time for body and mind to heal;
rejuvenate from a physically, mentally or emotionally
punishing task, or schedule, that brings
aching mind and body to a crash point.

Down times for me came at the
completion of directing plays,
or submitting semester grades,
or finishing summer stock.
The week after, I always felt
like I was walking in water up to my waist
with my brain sputtering along like a car
running on watered-down gasoline.

There comes a time when too much down time
builds stress, anxiety, and guilt
eating away at mind and body,
creating a malaise to the point that another
down time is needed to
rejuvenate from the previous one.
Such a cycle of down time
after down time after down time
is dangerous to a person's well being.
Survivalists kick out of the cycle
and find a cause to latch on to.

On the one hand, Energizer Bunny people
drive me nuts with their high-keyed,
never sit down mentality.
On the other hand, downers take all the gusto
out of life with their eat and sleep regimens.

Somewhere is a balance between the two;
a kind of purposeful down time when the
mind and body can heal yet activity be sustained
which maintains purpose, direction.

RONALD M. RUBLE

        I have been at that balance point fleetingly,
        for short periods, but never as a lifestyle.
        I keep searching and hope
        I don't fly off the teeter-totter
        and bruise my sense of need

DREAMS

Daydreams
Night dreams
Sad dreams
Glad dreams

Try to forget dreams
Repeated dreams
Heated dreams
Wet dreams

Haunting dreams
Scared dreams
Celebration dreams
Libation dreams

You dreams
Old dreams
Me dreams
New dreams

Cry dreams
Shock dreams
Pastoral dreams
Why dreams

Fight dreams
Flight dreams
Love dreams
Hug dreams

Revenge dreams
Hopeful dreams
Wish dreams
Woeful dreams

Sour dreams
Beat dreams
Dour dreams
Sweet dreams

Impossible dreams

All begin when
reality wavers
in its tug-of-war
with the subconscious.

Driven

He addresses the keyboard
as if possessed, feverish.
The "clack," "clack," "clack," of the keys
beat out a steady stream
of symphonic tympani.
Ideas flow from mind to finger tips.
Occasionally he stops
to roll his shoulders,
then continues on.
His stomach growls
a cry of desperation.
He bites his lower lip;
looks at the monitor.
Minutes, then hours, pass by.
The vocabulary assembly line rolls on.

A mind is a dangerous thing;
his fills with images, experiences,
assumptions, dreams, longings, words,
ideas, fears, secrets, and knowledge
until the need to tap the melon
makes his head ache.
Stream of conscience gibberish
pours onto the screen.
"Get it out! Just get it out!"
the voice inside screams,
"Before they cut the cord!"

He no longer hears the
"clack," "clack, "clack."
The "cha-ching" of each word
reminds him of the check-out counter
at the grocery when he was a child.
His finger-tip ballet becomes
a thundering stampede.
He hears vibrant screeching
just before words collide
and carom off one another.
Cacophonous laughter and
cries of anguish punctuate
the depth and breadth
of his vocabularies.

His mouth waters for sustenance
but he cannot stop.

Minutes sprint by
on their way to nowhere.
He writes until the stream of
energy and thought dries up
as do wet footprints
under a scorching noonday sun.
Finally, the piercing, jolting screech
of the macaw is over.
He pushes the chair away;
shoulders and head slump
as if trying to separate from body.
He will eat and replenish,
sleep and recharge.
He will be ready
when the bell rings,
for the next round.

Echoes

Echoes in the dark;
as rolling thunder bounces off the hills
lightning flashes in the ebony sky
revealing the flight of the nighthawk.

As rolling thunder bounces off the hills
rain pelts a rhythmic beat
on the roof of the old shed
shielding the truck from the storm.

Rain pelts a rhythmic beat
as cattle huddle together
while dogs and cats dash
for cover under the weathered porch.

As cattle huddle together
cows moo a haunting lament
and the leaves in the tree tops shout
echoes in the dark.

"Be silent or let thy words be worth more than silence."
—Pythagoras

Essence

Have you ever thought about anything
for longer than just a few seconds?

Have you given your undivided attention
to a task, idea, or encounter?
When nothing exists but
the object, event, or place?

Go on. Close your eyes.
Furrow your brow. Wrinkle your nose.
You can do it.

Terrific. Congratulations.

What a relief.

For a second there,
I thought you lost your essence.

Exquisite

She took his breath away!
He gulped down his reaction,
stepped back, hesitant.
She was elegant; cultivated and charming
as she worked the large room
going from one to another,
making her way closer to him.
He was a country boy; not
flawless, impeccable, or meticulous.
He was rustic, edgy, unrefined;
with sweaty palms and holding his breath;
not worthy of her polish and glamour.
He released the air inside just
as she stepped in front of him;
offered her hand.
She wore light, almost faint makeup;
just enough to project her
delicate, elaborate perfection.
Her scent was of the meadow
at summer time.
He felt a blush invade his face;
he squirmed a bit and heard
a strange voice part his lips,
"Nice to meet you."
Her natural smile, dimples,
blue eyes weakened his knees.
The look in her eyes
held him captive.
He smiled as he remembered
that meeting some fifty years ago.
Had he the vocabulary then that
he had now, he would have handled
that moment much differently.
Well, maybe.

Eyes

I can look into eyes forever.
Irises change color
right in front of me.
The prankster plays tag in them.
I see goodness in there.
Animated discovery jumps out
and smacks me in the face!
Ornery flirtation shoots at me!
I watch joy and celebration
dance a jig.
Peace and serenity languish inside.
Reflective thought sits
patient and absorbing.
Lens focus and probe for more.
Vulnerability and danger hide in them.
Destruction and terror invade.
Rage and hostility crouched to vent.
Pain and anguish hang on pupils
as moisture collects.
I have patted them dry.
I have kissed them shut and awake.
I have talked to eyes all night.
When nothing is in there,
they unsettle me.

Fall Rain

A late October rain
falls from the dark gray sky.
The dulled, slightly acrid scent is
unlike the fresh bouquet of spring,
or the floral fragrance of summer.
The air is filled with an infinite number
of liquid missiles streaking downward,
exploding against everything in their paths.
Leaves fall looking like
sting rays diving for deep water;
not like mini-Frisbees sailing on air.
Forming layers on top of one another,
a mottled carpet is manufactured
before my eyes.
Partially nude skeletons
try to cover their vulnerability
with the leaves remaining.
Should trees be capable,
they would blush over
this public disrobing.

Flowers

Flowers punctuate nature's beauty.
Buds open in splendorous glory,
releasing their fragrances as is their duty;
bees on blossoms taking inventory.

Buds open in splendorous glory,
lush colored petals reveal opulent yields.
Bees on blossoms taking inventory
bringing a rainbow to gardens and fields.

Lush colored petals reveal opulent yields
releasing their fragrances as is their duty,
bringing a rainbow to gardens and fields.
Flowers punctuate nature's beauty.

"In three words I can sum up everything I've learned about life: it goes on."

—Robert Frost

Gathering

They are all shapes and sizes, these people;
housing a variety of bloodlines.
Each one unique in temperament,
experience, demeanor and sense of humor.

We gather because we are a family.
We celebrate holidays, birthdays,
weddings, and graduations.
We support one another in times of need;
lend a shoulder, a helping hand.
We nourish each other in times of want,
with hugs, kisses, food, and laughter.

We are a multi-textured tapestry;
bonded together with strong, bold stitches.
Photogenic, we are not known to shy from cameras.
We are generous and share our many gifts.

The house is infused with the aromas
of the living: colognes, perfumes, shampoos,
scented candles, and food.
I breathe deeply and hold onto the air
as if in hunger, desperate to absorb every speck
of enrichment, every morsel of nourishment.

Adults mingle and glide from room to room;
children bustle in and out,
ever hungry and restless it seems.
I see adults, whom I hugged when they were children.
I sit, partially swallowed by the stuffed chair,
and feel contentment and peace.

I close my eyes and allow my mind to retrace
my years back to when I was a boy,
accompanied by family, at peace and comfort
with everyone and everything in my surroundings.
Neither can I stop the smile that creases my face,
nor the warmth that comes from within
and anoints my body and soul.

We gather, capture and collect memories,
nourish our minds and bodies,
give thanks to God,
that's what my family does.

Gerunds
The *-ing* form of a verb.

He couldn't remember all the times he'd been sunburned; but he knew it happened too often. The hard part wasn't getting baked by the sun. That was easy. The tough part was in the healing: putting on the lotion afterward to help dissipate the blistering and the itching from the drying skin. The peeling usually revealed how deep the burn had gone. Learning his lesson was often a painful process.

The longer he lived, the more he realized that his life was like an onion: at times sweet, at times hot. Peeling off a wrong layer would bring him to tears. He kept adding layers for safety and protection, shielding and cloaking his sensitive nature. He became adept at masking his innermost feelings and thoughts behind facades. He spent more time dreaming and fantasizing, adventures great and small. He was insecure, shy, and afraid of making mistakes. He learned to hide, disguising and concealing those things which brought him discomfort.

He wrote about such things and secreted them away. He enjoyed writing, gathering his thoughts with pencil and paper. Writing was a private task. No one would be reading what he wrote, eliminating the vulnerability. Occasionally, on a selective basis, he found himself sharing something. The rest he guarded.

Girls in White

Winsome, yet almost haunting,
    their eyes reach to you
    and unsettle your spirit.
Visitors to my home are drawn closer
    to study this composition of two
    girls at the entrance
    to the smokehouse.

Photogenic young girls in white,
    contemporary, yet period.
Their fashions are not of this era.
Seasoned red bricks, green ivy, and
    whitewashed timbers complement
    ornate straw hats, lace-trimmed linen,
    and white stockings. They suggest a
    time when the pace of life
    was less hectic.

Pale silhouettes are as bound
    by their kindred spirits as is
    their beauty framed by the
    shadowy doorway in which they stand.

Unblemished, the camera's eye has
    captured their goodness and innocence.
They are connected by the love of the other,
    transcending family and blood ties.
The taller one gently cradles the
    vulnerable essence of the smaller.
They are comfortable together.
    All is right.

I look at these girls every day
    and discover more about myself.
They touch me in ways which stir
    my feelings. I am enriched.
My heart fills with the song of their greeting,
    as when they embrace me and
    call me uncle.

"I love the swirl and swing of words as they tangle with human emotions."

—James Michener

Green

Hundreds of men carried industrial-sized
lunchboxes with thermos jugs cradled in the lids,
filled with nourishment to sustain
them through their arduous days and nights.
Lunchrooms filled with bawdy jokes and laughter
as sweaty bodies devoured food
packed by soft hands which also caressed their brows
at the end of a long eight-hour shift.
They joked about being frivolous, big spenders,
too much partying, buying flowers or chocolates for the little lady,
toys and clothes for the fruits of their loins.
Ragtop convertibles and Schwinn bicycles were in
their driveways and television sets in their living rooms.
Houses filled with bounty and love.
Parking lots were filled;
products forged, stamped, assembled,
and packed for shipping 24/7.
American products made the American way.
Times were good.

*****

Men and women with lunch pails in hand
filed into the factory that had less bustle to it now.
They didn't have to worry about parking;
there were always open spots.
Lunchrooms weren't as jovial; silence
was often more prevalent than talk;
laughter only now and then.
They felt lucky to be there,
to have work and money coming in
to pay for the necessities: food
on the table, clothes on their backs
and shelter from the seasonal elements.
Third shift was but a skeleton crew;
first and second shifts ran about
sixty percent of full load.
They knew more cutbacks were coming
and talked with their spouses and offspring
about sacrifices that would have to be made.
Dickies, proud clothier of the working class,
would feel this crunch too.
The domino effect would touch them all.
Times were not so good.

*****

He faced the padlocked gate and
stared at the "Plant Closed" sign.
A long drawn out sigh reflected the
sadness, emptiness that chewed from the inside.
Weeds were growing in the cracks of the parking lot;
sprawling growth had taken over
the once manicured entrance way;
pane after pane of glass was shattered and he
noticed birds flying in and out.
He wondered if they nested over
his old work stall, raised families there.
He thought of his grandpa who talked
of the good old days, days of plenty
when the factory was the hub of the town;
of his father's words detailing family sacrifices
made when things got tough.
He curled his fingers around the rusting wire
of the cyclone fence and momentarily
hung there as if not grounded.
Tears formed in his eyes and
a knot crippled his throat.
Everything that made this a great plant
was gone, its brain, heart, arteries
and veins stripped out…an empty, broken shell remained.
This was the third factory to close down in his town;
an entire industry left in ruin with no
chance of reestablishment in sight.
The October air was beginning to smell of decay,
a fitting companion to the scene before him.
Natures chlorophyll factories were shutting down,
the workers going home for the winter.
Green was disappearing into yellow, red, and brown.
Bright multicolored foliage was soon to be stripped
from the oaks, maples, birch, beech, ash
to reveal their naked bodies clutching one another
while facing winter's freezing elements.
At least they would all be clothed again
in the spring, resplendent in their reawakening.
He didn't know if he could say the same
for him and his family.
He hoped they all stayed healthy,
that they would keep their meager belongings,
always have something to eat.

His grandfather and father always told him,
during his growing up years,
"Never fear, God will always provide."
His long accepted sense of faith
was wavering. He wasn't as sure now.
He could not stop the sobs that pushed
up and rolled over his lips.
He entered his car and sat behind the wheel.
Opening a rumpled brown paper bag,
he pulled out a sandwich…hesitated, then put it back.
He put the key in the ignition and swallowed hard.
Times were bad.
He could feel his green disappearing.

Guernica

Horrors of war
    Agonizing screams
        Insidious destruction
            Absolute chaos

Agonizing screams
    Raging fires
        Absolute chaos
            Dismembered bodies

Raging fires
    Insidious destruction
        Dismembered bodies
            Horrors of war

Gut

Hazy outlines created by streamers of sunlight
    filtering through the Venetian blinds.
Nature's winged glee club heralds the beginning
    of a new day; a triumphant euphony!
Dust particles sparkle in sunbeams invading
    the furrows of the bed.
Taut muscles quiver under the strain of the
    body stretch which ushers in a yawn.
Assertive feet hit the floor and the body tags
    along, hesitant in its uncertainty.
Organic mass rights itself, then settles, and
    slowly shuffles toward the doorway.
Momentary vertigo descends, but the whirling
    environment calms, and the ordeal ends.
Day is here and the course is set.
    It's gut check time; meet the demands head on.
Take a deep breath, trial and error is your guide.

"Appearance blinds, whereas words reveal."
—Oscar Wilde

Handprint

Some will see it as unsightly,
that which needs to be removed
as soon as is possible.
Others as a mark of
careless haste, an insensitive
gesture from the uncaring.

I see a print from the soiled hand
of a young person; not an infant
or small child…pre-teens, maybe.
The impression is clear,
reflecting a strong life-line…
one I hope has avoided the sorrows
of abuse, degradation, bullying…
the emptiness of loneliness,
tears from anger or hate…
one I hope will be filled with laughter,
joy, love, and personal success.
A signature, of sorts, of a
person with a full life ahead,
capable of rendering optimisms.
I see a break in the print lines
at the base of the thumb; a bit
ragged, pointing down toward the wrist,
like a scar from a wound
that seeped life's juice and
brought a tear.
I see a clear patch, void of print ridges,
on the third finger just above the second digit,
the width of a band-aid.
A recent occurrence to someone perhaps active,
possibly injury prone.
I see an indicator of a moment in time,
a documented proof of presence,
evidence of existence,
an exclamation delivered to me,
"Look! I was here!"

Have You Noticed?

Have you noticed children singing?
They sing from their hearts.
They sing forth with gusto,
for the joy of sound.

Have you noticed children dancing?
They step and sway
to the rhythms of their spirits,
for the freedom of movement.

Have you noticed children playing?
They give and take,
squeal and laugh,
for the challenge of discovery.

Have you noticed children creating?
They draw and paint,
invent and design,
for the thrill of expression.

Have you noticed children laughing?
They allow their imp within
to bubble out, cascade and
crescendo to mix with other imps.

Have you noticed their silences?
They watch and wait,
dream and make wishes,
hope and pray
for someone to stop and notice
their presence and potential.

Have you noticed the teardrops
teetering on their eyelids, ready to
create glistening streaks,
down soft tender cheeks
disfiguring their innocence?

Have you noticed the warmth of their hugs,
the sweetness of breath before the kiss,
the spirit in their eyes when
they know they are loved?

Have you noticed?

Highway

Walking the line;
the solid yellow stripe
which dissects the whole
into two halves.

The solid yellow stripe;
a seemingly endless trail
of primary color six inches wide
rolling up and down the countryside.

A seemingly endless trail
sending a message of danger
should one choose to cross it
without due respect for consequence.

Sending a message of danger
to the foolhardy,
the risk takers who are
walking the line.

Hoar Frost

The early morning sun
sparkles like polished diamonds
reflecting off the frozen crystals
accentuating spider webs;
branches, twigs and tall grass
brilliant white,
flower like and feathery.
Minute ice crystals linked arm in arm,
engulfing and covering
even the smallest of surfaces,
rendering the ordinary extraordinary,
the introverted extroverted;
splendid in its eye popping beauty.
Take the time to view it,
study it, appreciate it,
capture and digest it.
This is nature's jewelry which
cannot be locked up in a vault
or stored in a safe deposit box.
Hoar frost…a
delicate gift of beauty
for the mind and heart.

Honest Work

Like a well-oiled machine,
rhythmic and constant,
the shovel bites into the chunky pile,
lifts its load to the chute,
and coal rumbles into the ebony bin below.
Leathery hands, cracked and calloused
after hours of dancing with the oak handle,
direct the worn shovel back
to its pick-up place at the bottom of the pile
time and again until the dimpled
metal plates of the truck bed are
unobstructed and reflecting the noon sun.
Only then do the thick, rough-hewn hands
let go of the shovel to rub across
a coal blackened face framed
by unruly salt and pepper hair.
His eyebrows are like untrimmed hedgerows.
Deep forehead lines and slashing crows feet
intersect the hills and valleys;
sprawling ravines etch
a wide dimpled grin.

He rolls down the sleeves of his plaid jersey shirt,
tucks loose tails into his thread-bare bibs.
His laughter bursts through
tobacco-stained teeth,
tumbles over coal dust covered lips.
His breath momentarily suspends in the
cold air before dispersing with the breeze.
Powerful arms and thick body
lift the polished chute onto the truck,
slam the tail-gate shut.
"It's honest work, I sleep good at night."
He grins, enters the truck,
points the faded red GMC
toward the highway, waves goodbye.
My gaze follows the billowing dust
until he is gone.

Hugs

Hugs and kisses all around have been
a tradition I grew up with.
To this day, I hug and kiss my
grandchildren, children, siblings,
aunts and uncles, cousins,
nieces and nephews and friends.

Hugs carry with them the scents
and energies of the givers.
Hugs can be socially polite and
politically correct.
Hugs can be an expression
of forgiveness and of healing.
Hugs can convey sorrow,
recognition, protection, concern,
thank you, and love.

Unreturned hugs leave me hungry.
I love the hugs when you can feel your
energy being exchanged with the energy of the other.
That's a five course meal.
I love hugs that are given in waves and pulses,
when you can feel your spirit dance with the
spirit of the other.
That's a banquet.
I love hugs that last awhile; where you
don't want to let go; where you can't help
but add a caress, a bit of a back rub,
a look into the eyes of the other.
That's a dessert tray.

A person's ultimate goodness
can be shared in a hug.
Those that come from the heart
are the best kind.

"Without words, without writing and without books there would be no history, there could be no concept of humanity."
—Hermann Hesse

I Wonder

Is anyone aware of the
long-lasting joy a snowflake gives to me
before it liquidizes on the tip of my glove?

Does the green caterpillar supping on
the cabbage leaf ever fear of being
someone's dinner?

Do parasites ever knock before entering?

Does my reflection in a mirror
see a reflection back?

Do rancid odors take joy
homesteading in nostrils?

Do dust balls plan their congregations?

Does the life of a raindrop flash before its eyes
as it heads for a splashdown on earth?

Is that morsel of food caught between my teeth
there by accident, design, or desperation?

Are the birds flying overhead aware that
their droppings desecrate my new car,
populate berry thickets,
or soil Easter bonnets?

I wonder . . .
what is the gift a man can give
which equals that of a
woman giving birth?

Iceman

The wind pushed against him
trying to bend him back, force
him to a place he had just been.
Sleet stung his face like nettles,
a summer skin reaction out
of place and time.
His shoes fought for traction,
desperate, struggled to grip some
texture that would anchor him,
give him a momentary sense of place.
To no avail, he slid back
against the brick wall,
arms outstretched he hung
there as if fastened by Velcro.
Happy hour with friends
would have to wait.
The thirst that gnawed
inside him all afternoon
no longer a dominant force.
The skin on his face was
beginning to numb down.
His eye lashes were freezing
to the point where he could not blink.
He had a vision of being chipped
from the wall with an ice pick
to become a centerpiece on a banquet table.
A vision of thawing, melting, dripping,
seeing the white linen table cloth run red,
long crimson fingers reaching out
to those watching in stupefied horror.
Klinger would have taken delight
in such Sturm und Drang!

"All words are pegs to hang ideas on."
—Henry Ward Beecher

If

If I am not what I am, what would I be?
Perhaps a mongoose, titmouse, or wallaby.
If I am not what I would be, then what?
Perhaps a snake, hyena, or hickory nut.

And what if I am not what I should be,
does it matter beyond the family tree?
Will others' perceptions of my worth
chart my course here on earth?

If I am not what I think I see,
is it possible I am not me?
In this world do I have a place,
actually filling valuable space?

If I am not what I think I ought to be,
is it obvious for all to see?
Do those who waste the talents they've got,
erode and become what they are not?

If I am not what others think I ought to be,
has the concept of value deserted me?
If I struggle articulating my self esteem,
does it mean that I'm not what I seem?

Why do we languish over such thoughts,
if shoulds and coulds absorb the oughts?
If only philosophers, poets, and saints have the answers,
why have we musicians, painters, actors and dancers?

In the Flight of a Feather

Soaring high, buffeted between the clouds,
    we feel the thrill and excitement of our future.
The macrocosmic view dazzles the senses;
    the freedom and power of omnipotence
    mesmerizes the self beyond the
    ability to sense danger or finality.

Surface breezes hurl the soft tufts of the cottonwood
    toward the eagerly awaiting thicket.
Whirled dizzy, they are in bondage to the summer blizzard
    as the brambles pierce their progress and
    hold them prisoner, a reality of our present.
The microcosmic moment dulls the senses,
    the helpless and numbing captivity
    clogs the fibers of our being;
    human will, an enemy to the process.

Winds destroy and nourish life.
Lifetimes consist of windswept paths
    where determinism reigns....
Our fragile journeys, often erratic,
    full of courageous trials,
    moments of affirmation and sacrifice,
    are mirrored in the flight of a feather.

INFINITIVES

Most common are those verbs
used with the word "to."

To discover to learn to grow,
to read to understand to enjoy,
to agree to disagree to differ,
to hope to experience to enrich,
to caution to protect to reassure,
to forget to remember to do,
to hurry to hug to heal,
to crawl to walk to run,
to sing to dance to act,
to rock to roll to rhyme,
to share to enrich to appreciate,
to eat to drink to nourish,
to itch to scratch to relieve,
to relax to sleep to dream,
to refuse to hurt to destroy,
to reach to touch to soothe,
to laugh to cry to reveal,
to embrace to accept to forgive,
to listen to like to love,
to believe to rejoice to accept,
is to dare to be infinitive.

"In the world of words, the imagination is one of the forces of nature."

—Wallace Stevens

KALEIDOSCOPES

The philosopher ponders, "Who am I?"
    The poet replies, "I am."
Those in power retort, "Who cares!"

Crickets, noted for their chirping endurance,
    orchestrate the night.
It's a male thing.

Tending to seduce
    with sedulous care.
Holidays do that.

Tightly tucked sheets
    hold prisoner
the dreamscapes of night.

The "tac-tac-tac" of the typewriter
    fuels a free spirit
with clumsy fingers.

Breezes ruffle hair, cool skin,
    alert to danger, remind us of hunger.
Blow winds, blow!

Night into day
    and day into night;
the repetition never ends.

Crystal drops spatter hot concrete;
    they scorch, then evaporate.
Winter sorrow lasts longer.

Windows are panes
    reflecting the pain
of the lost or forgotten.

Imagine a world where
    centipedes are under
contract with Reebok or Nike.

The pond is full of diamonds today,
    corseted with virgin lilies.
"Water, make love to me."

Leaf Raker

He loved the fall of the year;
the beautiful red, yellow, plum, green marbled tapestry
turning landscapes into impressionistic masterpieces.
He hummed the season's anthem, "Autumn Leaves,"
as he prepared for this year's homage:
rakes, wheelbarrow, tarp, and gloves.
He tried to bury the 9-11 images
he carried with him from a year ago.

Four hours later, shirt and headband saturated,
hands sore, arms, back, and legs aching,
he emptied another load of nature's bounty at the curb.
He appreciated anew the dedication and unselfishness
of firefighters, law enforcement officers, and
good Samaritans who never gave up their search.

The glee of the season waned, he trudged to the backyard.
No aspect of his normal workday made his
heart race so, assaulted his body so,
or made him sweat as profusely
as did that terrorist attack which stained his country.

Red splotches on his hands announced the
inadequacy of his gloves and the
virginal quality of his violated palms.
People with a mindless passion and a
passionless mind raped his country that September day.

A patriotic urgency and determination fueled him.
November's chill and diminishing light would drive him inside soon.
He wanted to do his part to restore order and pride.
His thoughts were of healing, of hard work, of
his need to demonstrate acts of freedom and peace again.

"Papa, potatoes, poultry, prunes and prism, are all very good words for the lips."
—Charles Dickens

Life Is...

"Patter-pat, patter-pat;"
raindrops plunk the porch portico
sheltering pecks of potatoes and prunes.
Poppies and peppers pirouette
as poplars parody the postures
of promiscuous professions.
Meanwhile, pompous people peep from
behind presumptuous papers preying on
prolific procedures of pure posh!
Life is ploddingly pedestrian.

"It's the words we whisper to ourselves that make us who we are."

—Marty Rubin

Logan's Creek

He had been coming here for some time now; this was his spot. His father and older brother brought him here when he was younger. He figured, they didn't like it as much anymore, but he continued to make the short bicycle trip on his own. He would race down the narrow pathway running beside the water, peddling as fast as he could, hitting roots and small rocks which threatened to throw him over the handlebars. The thrill of danger ran down his tingling spine and made him laugh. Low branches would lash out at him trying to steer him off course, brush him into the water. He ducked low, pumped harder. Into the meadow he rolled. The air was cool against his sweating body and the wildflowers smelled better than anything else. He would always take a deep breath as if to dine on the fragrance.

He loved this place, especially when the creek was up as it was now. He sat on the bank and put his bare feet into the water. The cool water swirled around his toes and he loved listening to the babbling noise just slightly above him as the clear water worked its way down over the rocks.

He was twelve and spent more time alone, now that his older brother had a car and worked so he could make the payments. When the two of them came to the creek, they always had an adventure: skipping rocks, fishing, catching turtles, waylaying pirates, going on a safari, swimming at the bend. They would leave after morning chores, lunches packed, and return home for evening chores before supper. Logan missed time with his brother but had come to learn that his alone times could be special too, in a different way.

Alone, the spirit of adventure was not as strong, sometimes not present at all. There was now a kind of magical appeal for him. Quiet, serene he would focus on the sounds of nature, allow the sun to soak into his body, the tall grass on the bank become his mattress, the bubbling water become his music, and he would peacefully fall asleep.

The creek was also the place he would go to think; speak in whispers, sort things out that confused him or didn't seem right somehow. There were so many things he did not seem to understand; at least not to his parent's ways of thinking—things about school, friendships, chores, and girls. Once in a while, out of the blue, the answer would come to him and he would thank the creek. If the answer worked out, he would thank the Lord.

On this summer day, he slowly lowered his body into the refreshing water. Floating, with his face just below the water line, eyes open, he drifted and watched fish dart by, crawfish scurry under rocks, a turtle make its way toward the bank. The hot sun warmed his backside and he allowed his mind to take him wherever it wanted him to go. Like a log, he drifted down to the bend, the swimming hole. He never gave thought to the danger of being alone in deep water. He was safe here; this was his creek.

Loons

Their soft, high-pitched warbles
    echo across the misty morning waters
        of a placid golden pond.

Stately heads held high,
    the pair bob on ripples, massaging
        two small chicks between them.

Mutual surveillance marks daily ritual
    as they warily tolerate the presence
        of invaders of their kingdom's court.

Aquatic clowns in search of breakfast,
    these great northern divers of the Midwest
        do so with a dolphin's grace.

Lifelong mates team-teach their offspring
    the often harsh lessons of life
        among the small islands of the pond.

They serenade a haunting melody,
    an anthem of peace and privacy,
        these speckled jewels of nature's domain.

Magic

The split second it takes for eyes to bulge open
on a child's face at the moment of discovery.
The tone in a voice that
melts away your fears and puts you at peace.
The beautiful rainbow inside the water drop
hanging from the lip of the old pump.
The instant when you feel for certain
you've been at this place before,
yet you know for a fact that you have not.
The salivation in your mouth that comes
from walking by a bakery and
seeing pastries through the window.
The electrical charge that surges through your body
when the coaster zooms down its deepest drop.
That ever so slight soft touch between
a boy and girl that makes them quiver.
That feeling you get inside you when
you watch a baby sleep.
That look in another's eyes that
increases your heart beat and
renders you a blithering idiot.

Magic moments make life great.

Masks

The masks of life are plentiful.
We hide behind the painted expressions of anger,
hate, pity, fear…sorrow, joy, happiness…
of child, adult, and parent.

Actors know masks and understand what works.
They cry through the comic, laugh through the tragic.
When successful we hold our breaths
to feel the hairs ripple our surfaces.

We cannot stop the gasps, laughter, or droplets
that irrigate our cheeks and
threaten to flood our consciousness.

Masks are necessary.
Actors penetrate their featured facades;
with laughter, sorrow, rage, and joy
they escape from behind their elegant edifices.

Painful, piercing shards shred our imprisonment,
demand of us to explore the depths,
the parameters which construct our beings
to season our souls.

Melting Images

Clarity of thoughts bring forth
sharp images of an experience.
The elements artists employ to
make their statements,
some at rest for static study,
others in movement for transitory study,
derive from both studies providing
care is taken to be receptive.

Missed interactions,
often produce melting images
of intentioned clear visions.
The exquisite detail
of a Michelangelo sculpture, or
Hopper or Wyeth painting,
runs and blurs to take on features
as if painted by Dali, de Chirico, or Picasso.

When not careful, meaningful
images can become as obscured
as are the works of Hofmann, Pollack
or Rothko, with subject matters
difficult, if not impossible, to discern.

My Freezer

A damp, cool, heavy mist descends to
embrace my shell draped upon
the scarred, weathered oak slats,
laced with carved epithets, and
proclamations of togetherness
imprisoned in crude Valentine hearts.
Nestled some distance between dim luminaries,
dancing shadows walk across to me as if trying to
massage the knots which engage my body.
This park bench, at the abyss of midnight,
is the perfect place to ponder; to
feel the north breeze and hear
the waves lap against the rocks.

"Son, death is a fact of life.
You have to learn.
Boys don't cry;
a pet is not a person.
Save your tears for people."
Dad turned and walked away.
I wanted to shout at him, but I didn't.
Laddie was people, to my brother, sisters and me.
I couldn't stop the tears that ran
down my cheeks and watered my shirt.
Our beautiful collie was gone and the
guy who hit him didn't even stop
his truck to see if he could help.

He saw his job as being
to toughen me up.
I was too soft said
this brother of mine.
Our sibling rivalry years
were filled with daily tests
of macho-hood,
one-upmanship and
painful retaliations,
by older over younger.
"I hate you!" I
shouted at him.
"You're bigger than me! It ain't fair!"
I cried on the outside from

hurt and frustration;
from betrayal and alienation.
My inside tears were from
the pain in my heart from my lie:
I loved him dearly.

"You need to focus on the tasks at hand.
You are more than capable
of doing good work.
I suggest you give a better effort,
young man, or you'll come
to regret the results.
Do you hear me?"
She returned to her desk
parting the sea of classmates' laughter
as Moses parted the Red Sea.
The way her rear end danced
inside her print dress;
the way her perfume hung in the air,
gently slapping my face
wave after wave;
the way her dark eyes flashed
when she stressed a point;
the way her breasts reached to me
when she leaned forward;
all reminding me of the extreme
difficulty of being a better student.
I never learned to fancy homework
the way I fancied her.
I never got a rise out of the study of
algebra the way I got a rise
in my loins studying her.
She was the sound, scent, vision and
fanciful dreams of my fourteenth year.

I was never a fighter;
not tough enough,
or cold enough.
In most cases, I was able
to melt the ice by being a clown.
I ran with the ice cubes at night,
and learned to play the role of
an ice cube during the day.
I lived with deceit because
I loved going to school.

I liked the kids in the class of 1958.
We laughed a lot,
bragged a lot, and
did the sock-hop routine.
My teachers saw in me what I did not,
what I wouldn't allow myself to see.
They chipped away at my ice façade.
They pushed me and I resisted.
They taxed me and I grumbled,
all the way to college.

I didn't belong here, in college.
Every day seemed to demonstrate
that fact to me.
I wasn't as tough, or as smart
as I thought I was.
I had never worked so hard, for so long,
fighting sleep deprivation,
headaches and sweaty palms,
for such lousy results.
I was the rat in the maze, the
hamster in the wheel running
madly but getting nowhere
that made any sense to me.
The thought of disappointing all
those back home,
who sacrificed so I could be here,
petrified me.
A lack of preparedness for this
higher level of expectation and
acquisition kept me from
pleasant dreams at night.
My brothers intervened;
showed me how to drop my façade,
how to chip away the ice,
how to laugh and cry, how
to appreciate the value and worth
of myself and of others, how to
trust my gut instincts and my talents.
My love of acting became a path.
Study skills, personal discipline,
a desire to excel, a support system
of care and concern were
the lasting gifts from my fraternity
and the theatre program.

The Greek way and footlights
fashioned my Dean's List status;
saved my bacon.

The general shook his head
side to side and muttered,
"You're too sensitive, wear
your feelings on your sleeves.
It's not the military way.
Got to toughen up;
plug your freezer in!"
He chewed on his foul-smelling cigar
and bored holes through me
with steely blue eyes.
"We're people, sir. Not machines.
People make mistakes, sir."
I squeezed out my response.
"Son, you're a sharp officer.
But you're too soft.
No place for soft in the service.
You'll be raw meat in the military grinder
and come out sausage,
all tied up in little links.
Get tough, or be in for
miles of pain!"
The military way of life
was frustrating for me;
didn't seem honest
most of the time.
My time came to exit;
I did so with no regrets,
before the grinder got too much of me.

"This is one of the worst papers
I have ever had to read!
This is not graduate level work.
This is pure crap!
Frame each page of this paper
and hang it on your wall
as a reminder of how not to write."
He was the butcher,
an academic hamburger maker, a grinder
preparing me for America's
best-selling sandwich filler.
He had ice in his veins.

Tears began to form; I couldn't stop them.
I disliked this professor's manner of
critique and personal demeanor;
his superior, God-like attitude;
his swaggering walk.
I worked my rear end off in his class;
driven by his callous pomposity.
I was bound to prove that
I could produce quality work.
I did, and in the end,
became a better writer.

My gut, heart, and mind told me
from the onset that we were
destined to become best friends,
somewhere down the line.
My first Playhouse summer
was my personal Renaissance.
I worked with him on sets
and with her as director to my actor.
We were as kindred spirits with
the same loves and approaches
to our craft and art form.
For almost forty years we
have grown up together with our families
intertwined in a variety of ways.
We have experienced and witnessed
success and frustrations,
trials and errors,
tests of our faith and health,
and family losses.
We play and work together
acting, choreographing, directing, teaching,
and continue to laugh, most of the time.
She is my Sis and he is my Bro;
we are works in progress and
dream of what we can yet become.

She had a working freezer:
ice cubes by the buckets,
this boss of mine.
"It's my way, or the highway!"
I suggested she lighten up
at a moment of aggravation,
and watched the veins in her neck

bulge to the bursting point.
She shot venom at me!
Pencils hurled in my direction.
The concussion from her door
being slammed shut assaulted
eardrums like grenade bursts.
Her presence pounded the joys
of work into submission.
She spoke of humanism; of care,
compassion, sensitivity, and love.
Her actions revealed little of these.
She was an ice machine.

"Till death us do part."
Straightforward are these words.
Simple and direct in theory;
first to lose significance in reality.
My sons filled the house with
joy and excitement most of the time.
To look into their eyes was
to fall in love all over again.
Their growing up years were
spiced with laughter, adventure,
discovery, trial and error.
With impatience and defiance
we three were pricked
by the thorns on the roses.
I most hated punishing them.
I knew the principles I
wanted them to learn,
but struggled with how best
to pass them on.
My mistakes were carnivorous.
They lacerated my heart,
dined on my insides,
swallowed my stamina.
I remember thinking that I had
most assuredly ruined them for life.
I feared most becoming cold,
uncaring, insensitive, or detached.
They fed on my fears.
I needed help; wanted a partner.
I knew that wasn't to be.
With pillow between knees and face,
I often muffled my tears of

doubt, insecurity, and loneliness.
I wasn't a good icemaker.

As is true with parenting,
there is no true way to know
what being a grandpa is about;
until you get there.
What ice I may be able to muster
up now and then gets
melted quickly by my grandchildren.
My sons, daughters-in-law, and
grandchildren give me more love
than I could possibly have imagined.
I cannot envision my life without them.
They keep me grounded,
keep me from falling through the ice.

Throughout my life
my most difficult work
has been to balance.
My achievements and failures will
continue to be tested by time;
passing the mantel on,
generation by generation.

Sitting on this bench, I codify
what I have known for over fifty years:
my freezer does not make ice.

Nervous

Who hasn't been agitated by the "nervy"
behavior of some people?
Those irascible types who
think they know everything,
have the right to do anything,
no matter the inconvenience or
discomfort their actions may bring?

The brazen audacity some people have
to push your buttons to find out how
to locate your sensitive point then
exhibit joy at your discomfort.

My stamina is wearing down.
I have less patience and
sensitivity toward those types.
I am unsettled because
I'm becoming nervous
with the nervy.

Night Symphony

Male crickets chirp their intentions
from the lush, thick, grassy banks
embracing the feeder stream.
Bubbling water percolates over
smooth rocks before cascading
into the pond below.
Gravel crunches underfoot
on the lane bordering the water.
The basso bravura of the bullfrog
slices through the mist hanging over the surface.
High-pitched squeaks echo from braces,
rubbing metal poles securing the floating dock.
Ripples lap softly against the
skin of the rowboat moored there.
Nasal beats of the diving nighthawk
mix with the muffled hoot, hoot-hoot,
of the sentinel owl on the hill above.
A contented sigh from the kneeling boy
produces the final soothing note;
a natural orchestra finely tuned.

Night Time

Crisp, cool sheets cover us,
    refreshing our togetherness,
        as we lay skin to skin,
            in our *nirvana*.

She sleeps quietly,
    rolled up protectively
        against the cold, and
            her intimate fears.

Contentment swells her nostrils,
    as she breathes and seals
        her eyes and lips,
            as she dreams.

I hold her close,
    half guarding and half
        possessive in my role
            as partner and lover.

I hurry to sleep,
    so I can rush awake
        to say, "Good morning!"
            and hear her say, "Hi!"

No Choice

"I had no choice!" I guess there is some truth here. I believe there are better choices than others. Thought should be given to selecting the best choice of those available. However, there are certain things in our lives that we have no choice over; some choose to lament those.

We do not get to select our natural parents. Our natural brothers and sisters, grandparents, aunts and uncles, cousins, should we have them, are not a matter of our personal choice. They are inherited entities. We neither have a choice over our birth gender nor our birthday. One can choose not to celebrate a birthday but the birthday will arrive on its own. Gender can be changed at considerable expense financially, physically and emotionally, but our birth gender will always remain the same. Our birth eye, hair, and skin color occurs without our choice. Of course, we can resort to cosmetic alterations should we not like the original versions.

We have no choice over releasing bodily waste except for the when and where; we can hold them in, with increasing discomfort, but sooner or later there will be a discharged elimination. Drinking and eating are not matters of choice if we want to live; only the what, where, when and how much are choice considerations.

Our religions are also inherited entities, at least in the beginning. In our formative years we tend to discover and experience the religion which influenced our parents and their parents. Our education and schooling are not generally matters of personal choice. Laws require some form of schooling, up to a certain age. Where we attend school is dependent upon a proximity to where we live, unless we have the financial means and are willing to pay tuition to enroll with a district elsewhere.

Taxes! The penalties of getting caught evading taxes are severe. Of course we can avoid paying taxes should we be willing to accept the punishment for being caught doing so.

Death! Avoiding death is not a matter of choice. Medicine can delay the inevitable but I know of no one who has succeeded in living forever. While we may be able to exercise choice on the where and when of death, death remains a certainty.

I am sure that deeper thought may give rise to additional instances of "no choice" situations. We need to focus on the choices we have, accept responsibility for the ones we make, and move on.

"To me, the greatest pleasure of writing is not what it's about, but the inner music that words make."
—Truman Capote

Nocturne

Orange and yellow spirits
gently dance to and fro,
anchored to embers,
choreographed by the breeze.

Crickets, nestled in deep grass,
sing their desires,
pleading for close encounters
of the right kind.

Soft smoke ascends into twilight,
to embrace descending fog;
filtering pink streamers
slicing through from the west.

A cool, damp air blanketing
retiring and awakening life forms;
temperature slowly falling,
altering the aroma of the night.

Nouns

Nouns are wonderful words.
We know them as the names
of persons, places, or things.

Our alphabet is resplendent with nouns
beginning with every letter.
Take the letter "f":
some of the more imaginative nouns are
factotum, festoon, fiddlehead, fistula,
Flintstone, frontier, fuchsia and fungi.
The letter "k" gives us kazoos, kennels, kiosks,
koalas, Kris Kringle, knockwurst and kumquat.
The often quixotic "q" rewards us with quagga,
quarantine, quarry, Queen Anne, quiver, and quotation.
Selections from the letter "s" include
samovars, sapsuckers, Shakespeare, shoemakers,
snipes, sorority, spigots, and superstitions.
The letter "z" is no slouch either
with zany, Zeus, zipper, zombies,
zoos, zwieback and zygotes.

Nouns are fun to pronounce
and rely on frilly adjectives for full fruition:
fanciful follicles,
kindly koalas,
quivering quivers,
slimy sapsuckers, and
zappy zombies.

Old Barn

Barn and silo built with sweat and blisters.
I wonder about the people who farmed there,
if they ever danced in that barn,
played music there, ate lunch there,
if Halloween parties were hosted there.
Did it have a granary, a milk parlor, a hay fork lift?
What hopes and dreams were held captive there?
How many coats of paint did it receive?
How many baby animals were born in it?
I wonder if it had a basketball hoop
attached to one of its beams;
if kids played beam tag in it;
if forts were built in its hay mows
and over-nights held there.
Did a lover's union ever take place in there?
Did snakes catch mice in it, owls eat snakes there?
I wonder if a little boy stood in the middle of it,
looked up and shivered with excited awe
over how big it was and he so small.
Did terrible accidents happen there,
sorrow or hate grow there?
I wonder how grand it looked before
time and weather cracked its seams.
Might it have been built
on the same site as an earlier barn
lost by fire or disabled by time?
I have never been inside it, though it beckons me.
I feel connected and long to touch it;
to have its stories race through my veins.

Ornate

Each photograph was stunningly beautiful. I
marveled at their lavishly bold colors and shapes,
strong structures, their flashy public flair. Great
madams, I thought.

> Their flamboyant lines, ornamental accessories,
> elaborate detail, made me think of food. They
> were almost edible, a grand buffet.

These painted ladies were manicured, had charm
and character; a lived-in look. I thought about
all the stories they could tell; the people they had
been with, watched eat, seen dressed in all their finery,
seen undressed. The holiday festivities they had lived through.

> No doubt they had housed every conceivable
> emotion, thought, and deed. That thought gave
> them a delightful sense of mystery.

Baroque havens. Architectural splendors,
    each a painter's masterpiece.

Over

    This word may well have the most creative usages of any word in our language. My childhood was often confusing to me and "over" was one of the reasons. How could the same word possibly be used to convey something that was across, finished, and yet also be appropriate for above, exceeding, on top of, more than, beyond, and aloft? My mind did not want to accept that the same word could be used for "Red Rover come over," and "the cow jumped over the moon."

    I was both amazed and perplexed that usages for the word increased tenfold when used as a prefix. I experienced dreary, dark, dull gray overcast skies; arrogant, domineering, dictatorial overbearing acquaintances; late, tardy, beyond the deadline overdue books; burdened, oppressed, saddled, weighed down, overloaded with homework; as well as overshadowed and overhauled by those who outshined, dominated, passed me by, and eclipsed my shyness of being overweight.

    My years as a parent brought me face to face with overpowering apprehension about doing the right thing; how to overrule and oversee the desires and needs of my sons without overthrowing and overriding their growth and potential. Many times I found conflict between their priorities and mine. How should I react to their blunders, lapses, neglect, slip-ups and oversights with their daily chores? And, being a single parent, who would countermand, invalidate, reverse, and overturn, or overcome my errors in judgment? I had to discover ways to disregard, forget, let pass, pardon and overlook those things which bothered me in some overflowing way without stunting their exploration and discovery.

    I have to admit to times when I felt bowled over, confused, deluged, devastated, engulfed and overwhelmed by my responsibilities as a person. I have had many moments when I became agitated, beside myself, emotional, frantic, tense, worked-up, and overwrought by the expectations that confronted me.

    Now, looking back, generally speaking, on the whole, by and large, and in the long term, my life, overall, has been enriching and forgiving. I am delighted, euphoric, jubilant, tickled pink and overjoyed about that!

"Poetry is the rhythmical creation of beauty in words."
—Edgar Allen Poe

Pas de Deux

Ah, to watch a *pas de deux*!
Bodies full of zest and zeal,
lithe expressions in full view,
spirited dancers with great appeal.

Bodies full of zest and zeal,
with grace and charm displayed on cue.
Spirited dancers with great appeal,
moving in colors of every hue.

With grace and charm displayed on cue,
lithe expressions in full view,
moving in colors of every hue.
Ah, to watch a *pas de deux*!

Past Participles

If I do, then I can say I did,
and brag about what I have done.

"Please choose me," he begged.
So she chose him and within minutes
he understood what it was like
to have been chosen.

They didn't know what to wear.
They wore nothing yesterday,
and that has been worn too often!

He invited his friends for a drink;
they drank and drank and drank,
until it was clear they were drunk!

She wanted to sing again,
so she sang until all had been sung.

He wished he had known then
that all he had come to know
he essentially knew already!

The poet sat down to write.
Later he read what he wrote
and laughed at what he had written.

Path

My inability to accept the temporary nature of my being is devouring the marrow that is essential for my very continuance. You and I, we are what we are, do what we do, because of the need to make a statement unlike that made by any other. The mortal qualities of those who birthed us, gave us life and helped construct our identities jars us, knocks us back to reality on a plane we do not want to confront it on. We know the lurking pangs of emptiness are not fantasies, those which auger into the blackness of one's soul rendering insight and logic into tar-babies writhing in pools of pitch, choking their cries for freedom. So we continue the fight because we know we can go further than Sisyphus—to arrive at that spot, void of previous intervention, and make claim to the circle which defines our place. Centered in the spotlight where we belong, we face the world's auditoriums and with grand elegance of body and voice proclaim, "I am!"

We bask in the grand echoes washing over us in waves. Each "I am" rolls over us with more might than the one before. We squat in the ancient tradition, nourished and enriched by the ritual, the process, the evolution which makes us whole. We insist the journey be on our terms, within our time frames, and orchestrated by the uniqueness of our identities. We often face vertigo when something, not a part of our design, intrudes upon our quest. We become humbled in a way we find confusing and frightening...we grieve in unfamiliar paradigms searching for the embrace that heals and rights our course.

Our Jacob's ladder is there, we've earned the right to climb to infinity. We know our mothers, fathers, anyone we've ever loved and lost, who've made the climb before us will be there. We reach out, unsteadily, infant-like, praying that a hand will meet ours and lead us into the spotlight, our promised land, comfort place, home. At war with restlessness, the climb feels awkward, full of uncertainty. The hunger for a place of serenity, peace and fulfillment spurs us on. Perched on gossamer wings, we drink nectar from the ornate fountain and feel the refreshing liquid pump life back into our being.

"All our words are but crumbs that fall down from the feast of the mind."

—Khalil Gibran

Ponderables

Half-assed, half-cocked, half-empty,
    halfhearted, half-mast, half-pint;
what is wholeness?

Sharing, caring, embracing,
    understanding, supporting, caressing;
sensitivity or calculated petting?

If "getting popped" means to be shot,
    is the killer a popper and
the victim a poppee?

Does the steaming macaroni in the colander
    know it's to be drenched in an acid
bath, then masticated?

Are the mice scurrying in the wall,
    six inches from my pillow, aware their
play sparks a story in a child's mind?

Hellbender, hellbent, hell-cat,
    hell to pay, hell or high water;
serious trouble or poetic license?

Cherry PEZ, duck tails, pinky swears,
    switchblades, and "Rockin' Robin."
Was there ever such a time?

A stream of grapefruit nectar, an impudent
    youngster, a thin spray from a hose,
an undersized kid. All squirts?

Life cycle, life-giving, lifeline,
    life of Riley, life-on-the-edge, and lifespan;
all matters of lifestyle?

High-backed chrome-plated swivel stools
    address the cool marble counter top;
soda fountains, symbols of opulence?

Imagine a world free from pain, disease,
    hunger, or sorrow.
Would we become insensitive beings?

Prepositions

Words that combine with a noun, pronoun,
    or noun equivalent to form a phrase.

For as long as recorded time
    the seasons have been with us.
As soon as we dispense with one,
    another initiates itself,
by virtue of and according to
    the master plan

In order to appreciate a season,
    we give thanks to its singular beauty.
Each change constitutes a right of passage,
    which we spend nourishing the self,
in accordance with experiencing
    the master plan.

Regardless of the pressures of our day,
    we take time for the present.
With a view to what we feel from within,
    we anxiously look towards tomorrow,
pursuant to living with respect
    to the master plan

We may grumble from time to time
    about this season or that;
in spite of ice, snow, rain, and heat,
    we take the days in stride.
We endure the weather when we are together
    on behalf of the master plan.

"It does not require many words to speak the truth."
—Chief Joseph

Quandary

We all have states of doubt;
have we done the right thing?
Being a Romantic by nature
but an organized disciplinarian
by design often creates a
dissonance in me that is
extremely difficult to overcome.

Questions

Did you ever think,
when I was a child,
that I would grow up
to be meek or wild?

Did you ever snicker,
then think twice,
if I would be
naughty or nice?

Did you ever wonder,
along the way,
if things would turn out
to be okay?

Did you ever say,
within your mind,
I have some doubt,
what he will find?

Did you ever believe,
that I would grow,
and find a place in
life's great show?

Did you ever give me,
a second look,
and wonder if I might
write a book?

Did you ever wonder,
when you looked at me,
what you got was
more than you could see?

Did you ever imagine,
in me back then,
the gifts that have taken me
where and when?

Quick

No one has time anymore;
things must be done now, in a hurry.
We try to put six hours into every four,
make sure there is time for a last second flurry.
Speed over quality seems to work best;
the time of the process becomes the real test.

Quick assets- ATMs
Quick breakfast- juice or coffee
Quick contacts- cell phones
Quick cooking- microwave dinners
Quick freeze- a stare or vocal tone
Quick fix- speedy solutions
Quick grasp- hasty understanding
Quick information- instant messenger
Quick meals- the drive-through
Quickie- hasty sex
Quick review- fifteen seconds or less
Quick step- on the run
Quick stop- two minutes or less
Quick tempered- hair trigger emotion

We have become products of
the "quick" reality.

"Much wisdom often goes with the fewest of words."
—Sophocles

Ronald M. Ruble

Quit

"Quitters never win and
winners never quit!"

Is this true
for those who
consider suicide,
have method in hand,
but cannot commit the deed?

"Words are, of course, the most powerful drug used by mankind."
—Rudyard Kipling

Rancid

Hot searing pain exploded deep within;
his screams pierced chaos and invaded
the marrow in his bones.
"No. Not now." his voice rasped,
a desperate plea to be heard.
"The job isn't done!"
He saw himself wobbling side to side,
his legs unable to support his body.
He sank slowly into the rancid mud.
Breath shot from his mouth before
oozing filth saturated his clothes.
His life force streamed from him,
red syrup running into butterscotch pudding,
pulling him further into the black
forbidden zone he'd had cold sweaty
dreams about time and again.
"Mama. Papa." he groaned, "I'm sorry...."
Silence...stillness bathed the steaming clearing.
His sacrificial contribution in this rancid war,
his courageous and unappreciated work done,
so very far from home,
in a war we could not win...
did not win.

"A torn jacket is soon mended; but hard words bruise the heart of a child."
—Henry Wadsworth Longfellow

Rebuke

Teddy had been yelled at, lectured, and
scolded many, many times.
Today was no different from any other
during his eleven years.
He was accepting of admonishment
from others.
He abdicated any sense of
assertiveness and assumed the
whipping-post position.
Why do anything different,
he thought,
it would not change a thing.
Losers will always be losers;
not worth anything except to be
the objects of abuse by others.
Teddy learned to live with himself
by acquiring the attitude that his place
on earth was to be an absorber of
hate, anger, pity, and fear.
He had been branded by rebuke.
The flashlight beam glistened off
the blade as he brought
it to his wrist.
"I'll teach them,"
he whispered.

Reminders

I walk slowly to the house, uncertain.
    Feeling tired, I sit on the edge of the porch
    and look down the now empty street.
    It is just me now; the silence in the
    house will be deafening.

My thoughts turn to old newsreels in my mind,
    a montage of images in motion: romping
    with my sons in the backyard; hearing giggles
    of young boys during a sleepover, well past
    their quiet time; rocking a fevered boy cradled
    in my arms; the angelic faces of sleeping boys;
    a gentle caress of a tear-stained cheek; kissing
    a boo-boo to make the pain go away; tickling writhing
    masses of tears and joy; watching them hang their
    ornaments on the Christmas tree; of
    snow-angels on a January morning.

I long to relive the moment, when hand in hand, my
    young sons pull me forward, ever closer to the
    front door, screaming with animated excitement,
    "Come on Daddy! Hurry! Hurry! It's safe in here!"

My sons remind me of why I am here.

Resplendent Tapestry

I know of no time of the year
which is prettier than that of fall.
Varied earth-greens mesh with
red, yellow, and orange.
The brilliant blue, jewel-like sky
in contrast to the rainbowed carpet below.
The bright morning sun illuminates
the treasure for all to see
as minds and spirits dance with glee.

With each passing fall,
I become increasingly conscious
of the dancing of leaves in the air,
of the sizes and shapes which mark
the identities of their splendid hosts.

I have fond boyhood memories
of standing on top of Mt. Jeez and
looking out over the valley below me,
viewing multicolored tapestries like no other.
While I knew nothing of impressionism then,
the scene was fitting of the visions of Renoir or Monet.

The good Lord certainly did His job well;
He got it right the first time.

I have entered the autumn of my life
and pray my journey will be as striking.

Roads

I grew up walking the small dirt and gravel roads that typically served as the conduits connecting families, farms, small towns, and ways of life in rural Ohio. I remember warm summer's dust kicking up around my bare feet, mud squishing between my toes after steaming rains. In the spring and fall, mud sloshed up my boots and attacked my pant legs. In the winter, Dad tried to avoid the frozen ruts which would trap tires and add swerving excitement to the ride. Such roads were often so narrow that we had to pull over to the side in order to allow an oncoming car to pass by.

Summer's dust coated the roadside greenery in a yellow-brown comforter. The washboard surfaces made the car rattle and bump and Dad would slow down, reluctantly, at Mom's urging. Hot breezes carried the light brown air onto white sheets drying on the line. I could feel the grit in my teeth. Seasonal mud got tracked everywhere and increased Mom's washing dilemmas on a daily basis. Frozen rain, covered by snow, made for wonderful sledding on the rolling roads close by. Back then, I had never ridden on a roller coaster but I enjoyed the hilly and winding roads that were our pathways. Almost everybody rode these country roads; there were few choices.

The two-lane, hard surfaced roads existed and were treats to travel. They provided a smooth ride, no dust to inhale, plenty of room for cars to pass by, and dizzying speeds. I remember the floating sensation that permeated my body when tires left dirt and hit blacktop. The head to toe tingling sensation caused by washboard conditions remained several yards down the smooth surface.

The dirt roads had little advertising. I remember seeing an occasional Allis Chalmers or John Deere farm implement sign, a feed and grain sign or two, and lots of handmade signs for the sale of vegetables, fruit, eggs, hay, straw, grain, night crawlers, minnows, and dough-balls.

The highways had large colorful billboards that featured the wares of Westinghouse, Tappan, Sears, General Electric, Maytag, Frigidaire, Philco, Zenith, Studebaker, Chevrolet, Wonder Bread, Coca-Cola, Dr. Pepper; signs of all kinds about every half-mile or so and clustered at intersections. We all enjoyed looking at and reading the variety presented.

The very best signs had to be the Burma Shave signs. I think they appealed to everyone; young or old, big or small, male or female. The easy to spot red and white signs featured four line couplets of a humorous nature.

They were spread far enough apart for easy reading with the last sign advertising the popular shaving cream, Burma Shave. While funny, they warned all of the dangers of poor driving habits. They were effective. Drivers knew about Burma Shave even if the quality of their driving may have been suspect.

My siblings and I always looked forward to those signs which also meant we looked forward to riding on those roads where they took up residencies. Easy to memorize, I remember the first one that stayed in my mind: "DON'T LOSE YOUR HEAD/ TO GAIN A MINUTE/ YOU NEED YOUR HEAD/ YOUR BRAINS ARE IN IT/ Burma Shave." I was seven years old, in the second grade, and the year was 1947.

Over the next years Burma Shave signs became one of the reasons for going anywhere…at least for me. Several of my favorites were: "CAR IN DITCH/ DRIVER IN TREE/ THE MOON WAS FULL/ AND SO WAS HE;" "DROVE TOO LONG/ DRIVER SNOOZING/ WHAT HAPPENED NEXT/ IS NOT AMUSING;" "A GUY WHO DRIVES/ A CAR WIDE OPEN/ IS NOT THINKIN'/ HE'S JUST HOPIN';" and "AROUND THE CURVE/ LICKETY-SPLIT/ BEAUTIFUL CAR/ WASN'T IT?" Such slogans became topics of conversation among my classmates. We all had our favorites.

Burma Shave also made it into my classroom. The teacher asked us to create our own verse and not copy one that was posted. I was so proud of my submission: "CAR ON ROAD/ BOY ON BIKE/ BOY NEEDS SPACE/ CAR TAKE A HIKE." I knew it wasn't as good as Burma Shave's, but I was only a ten-year-old kid.

I read somewhere that the last Burma Shave signs were taken down in 1965. Our two-lane country roads have not been the same. I miss that roadside verse in my life. I wish they would come back so I could enjoy them all over again. I cannot help but think that they would become as popular as they once were.

The roads I have traveled took me many places, in many states. I have walked some and driven many. Roads are threads of my fabric, Burma Shave a spice in my life.

Ruminate

"Well, that's the deal, Dalton."
"I don't know, Cable."
"You won't get a better deal."
"I don't like to plunge into things,
like to think on them awhile."

Three days later...
"Dalton, have you thought about it?"
"About what, Cable?"
"The deal."
"Still thinkin' on it."
"It's a great deal."

Two weeks later...
"Dalton, I need your answer.
We have to move on this."
"Don't rush me now.
You sure them figures is right?"
"They're right."

One month later...
"Dalton, I'm short of patience,
do you want the deal or not?"
"I understand. I'm still
mulling it over."

Another month later...
"How you doin', Cable."
"I'm doin' fine, Wyatt. Hi Seth."
"Hi Cable. Did you hear about Dalton?"
"What about him?"
"He died!"

Rustlings

Listen! Listen closely…hear the
rustlings of the leaves in the tree tops,
faint, but clear as the soft breeze
pushes leaf against leaf,
leaving branches and trunks still.

The sound is gentle, soothing as
if to foreshadow kindness and respect.
The breeze is high, caressing only the
tops of the tall oaks; I feel no movement
on my skin where I stand.

Should Greek mythology be true,
that the rustlings in the leaves of
the tall oak trees are a sign from the gods,
then today is going to be a good day;
a joyous and perhaps prosperous one.

There is no violence or anger in
the swing of these leaves,
no sharp pitching of branches and trunks
turning and twisting as if to be
splintered and broken by a strong force.

This leaf talk invites me to sit, look and listen;
to enjoy the squirrel perched upright on the limb
washing itself with vigor,
to watch butterflies flutter
in follow the leader mode,
to enjoy the smell of fresh cut grass
from my neighbor's lawn,
and to taste the tart lemonade
as it quenches my thirst.

Oh leaves, speak to me and I will listen;
soft breeze, sing to me and I will dance.

Seasonal Debris

Garbage bags stuffed with identifiers of what we are;
shrubbery clippings and rotting grass,
flying fowl splattering excrement from above,
earthworm carcasses cluttering concrete and pavement,
cottonwood tufts salting landscapes,
June bugs bouncing off of screens,
muffleheads infiltrating human hair,
dried mayflies crunching under feet,
mosquito infested puddles and ditches,
road kill baking in the sun,
forest fire soot and ash,
hail storms pelting out a beat,
bloated, maggot infested fish on the beach,
overflowing dumpsters cluttering the natural order,
soiled paper plates skipping across lawns,
flower petals losing their zest,
sun-bleached linen florals embracing gravestones,
school-colored confetti dotting bleacher seats,
toilet paper garlands hanging from foliage,
frost strangling life from entities,
falling swirling leaves,
cornstalks, dried husks, and candy wrappers,
remnants of ghosts and goblins,
smashed pumpkin shells,
garbage bags stuffed with mementoes of what we were,
sleet stinging delicate skin,
driving snow constructing drifts across roads,
used Christmas trees discarded for pickup,
silver icicles accentuating curbsides,
and stained, defiled snow.

Deterioration, rubble and waste
in the name of traditions, ceremonies, and nature.

Ronald M. Ruble

Shattered Windshield

The fragments of life
float eerily around me,
beyond my space.

I long to touch them,
to connect and bond;
they are beyond my contact.

My body aches and needles
pierce my skin at a thousand points.
A scream escapes and dances into space,
bombarding a private punishment.

Energy and will pumps from me
through gaps sliced into my body.
Red rivulets alter the interior design
of my creature comfort.

The bubbling of water and
singing of summer frogs
keeps me from nodding into night,
a disruption of pleasure.

Through the mist
come sounds of the living
streaking by above me
on the mountain road.

The stalled time of concentration
gives way to the whirling hour hand.
The red warning of morning
is splintered by the shattered windshield.

My tears flow from skin to air,
crystal drops floating free,
irrigating fractured moments
of my experience.

Smiles, frowns, laughter, and tears
orchestrate the ballet of family.
Friends and acquaintances celebrating
the moments of birth, life, and death.

*****
I can feel the joy of each hug
ever received,
the throbbing love
of each kiss ever delivered,
the pain and anguish
of each injustice ever administered.

God, this is not where
I envisioned my end to be,
a briar thatched ravine
in the middle of nowhere.
This is not the euphoria
I hoped for
when thinking of the end
of my time on earth.

One's death isn't meant
to be a moment alone
with no one there
to comfort the way.

"Someone's praying Lord,
come by here."
"Someone's dying Lord,
bless me here."
"Someone's ready Lord,
take me now."
"Oh Lord,
take me now."

My final awareness
is of the cobwebbed shadows
covering me gently as a baby's blanket
trying to hold me together
as I once was.

As the sun lit my tragedy,
darkness stifles the music,
dreams cease,
the mosaic fades,
my journey ends.

Shoes

My shoes talk
to me as I walk.
Each step brings forth
a squeak that comes
from stretching the pores of leather,
pores which cry out
in defiance from being
abused by weight and contortions
pressing them beyond their comfort zones.

When wet, the soles of my shoes
scream in high pitched wails.
Slip-sliding on tile floors,
molded treads project orchestral sounds
in discordant sharps and flats.

At night, at the end of a long day,
after birthing my feet,
their silence speaks of a well earned rest;
dutiful servants of custom and fashion.

So Many Times

There are so many things I don't know about,
questions I don't have answers for,
activities I haven't experienced,
religious differences not attended to,
flavors not tasted.
So many textures I have never touched,
events I haven't witnessed,
cultures I am ignorant of,
wraps I haven't pulled around me.
So many seconds, hours, and days wasted,
aromas not smelled,
sounds not heard.
So many opportunities missed,
chances that slid by me,
lessons not adequately learned.
So many memories flood through me,
of hearing your laughter,
seeing your eyes dance.
So many times you healed my wounded spirit
and enabled me to get back on track.
So many talks, on so many topics.
So many times we have shared our souls.
So many gifts you have given me,
so, so many times.

"For of all sad words of the tongue or pen,
the saddest are these: 'It might have been.'"
—John Greenleaf Wittier

Solitary

Birds frolic in the sun,
their chatter but a mime to me.
Trees move to a beat,
no rustle massages me.

A bumblebee floats errantly by,
its tiny engine does not speak to me.
The sprinkler dances to a fast tune,
no cascading cadence cloaks me.

Ambulances pass by on the street,
no piercing wails penetrate me.
Rains soak the outside,
there is no varying timpani for me.

A vacuum embraces my dilemma,
all I once had, now gone.
There is a world beyond this cell,
restraining my incarcerated remains.

With each jerk of the second hand,
the stillness of days and nights drag on.
Adrift on a mattress to nowhere,
silence measures my tolerance,
my thoughts on what might have been.

Sons

In a life filled with enrichment,
discovery, joy, and accomplishment,
my sons shine as the brightest
stars in the heavens;
they are the greatest gifts I have received.

They brought me my greatest responsibility,
apprehensions, fears, feelings of
inadequacy, delight, joy,
happiness, and completeness.

They make me feel whole,
fill me with pride and admiration.

My heart still skips a beat
when they call me dad or give me a hug.
They keep me grounded.
Life without them would
plunge me into an abyss,
an unfathomable chasm.

Such a thought unnerves me.
I want to see their smiles
and receive their embraces
again and again,
time after time.

Special People

I am blessed to have
wonderful people in my life.
They have been with me
at all crossroads,
at all venues,
at all trials and tribulations,
at all successes and celebrations.

They shared with me
their special gifts of advice, caution,
companionship, friendship, honesty,
hugs, experiences, innocence,
joviality, kisses, knowledge,
pep talks, truth, and wisdom.

Their gifts excited me, directed me,
supported me, scolded me, challenged me,
encouraged me, stopped me, massaged me,
upset me, prodded me, motivated me,
taught me, and led me to discoveries
about myself and others.

They are family members,
friends, loves, mentors,
students, supervisors, supervisees,
actors, artists, designers, directors,
writers, neighbors, children,
grandchildren, playmates, and workmates.

Their ages range from
infants to octogenarians.
They come from all
backgrounds and interests.
Their common denominator is
they are caring and loving.

I keep adding names to my list.
I am blessed.

Sycamore

Towering high above the houses,
some ninety feet or so I expect,
stands a mighty sycamore.
With a straight trunk and
symmetric silhouette,
this giant tree reaches to me
from across the street.
For over thirty years I have watched it
evolve through the seasons,
a majestic monument to nature,
to the great outdoors.
With its buttonball fruit,
mottled, marbled bark,
and broad sweeping leaves,
it commands the attention of all
who drive and walk the street.
Dressed in green splendor,
it sways to and fro in July breezes;
it stands tall in winter,
naked with nary a shiver.
I have played ball with
my sons and grandsons
in the shade of its canopy.
Three generations of my family
have raked its leaves,
which seem to sail the winds
and deposit onto my lawn,
leaves which measure broader
than the length of my hand
from longest finger to wrist.
Its October leaves remind me
of county fair fried treats,
elephant ears, with cinnamon sugar.
Leaves eavesdrop
on all conversations uttered
on my end of the block.
I wonder at the stories
this tree could tell.
I place the leaf gently against my ear,
hoping to hear a whispered secret.

Tears

Our very essence struggles to hold back the one
body fluid that is perfume for the soul.
Muscles and senses contract, twitch, and tremble
under strain of the fear of embarrassment
for this intimate baptism.
Tissue and fiber expand and
bulge under the burden.
Searing pain crowds our conscience.

With one last defiant surge of protest we
gurgle the threshold when
tears swell over the wall
as moisture from a lanced wound.
Crystal pearls cascade
over creamy smooth skin and
catch fire, prismatic as they
invade shafts from dancing flames,
leaving a thin wet trail skin to fabric.

Puny cleansers of life,
satin tributaries of the mind,
bubbling from pores of
the subconscious.

Unabashed
energy
from the
self.

Tender Times

We've all been told there's a time for everything.

A time for being with others,
    experiencing joy, celebration.

A time for being alone,
    experiencing loneliness, solitude.

Often, such times are the best times on earth…
    they are the tender times,

And it's only the *where* and *when* that counts.

I am free to play, sing, rejoice, or cry,
    to pen my thoughts!

Because, the *why* comes later.

"To get the right word in the right place is a rare achievement."
—Mark Twain

Then Again

He looked tired, worn out,
ready to give up on life
and the pursuit of happiness
that he knew was not coming.
Threadbare clothes hung loosely
on his thin frame as if recklessly
thrown onto a hall tree.
He walked aimlessly,
lurching point to point,
a silver ball in a pinball machine
operating in slow motion,
repelling from here to there,
somewhere, anywhere,
nowhere in particular.
I missed the sound effects
which tantalize, seduce the player,
sounds which set the
ambiance of busy arcades.
Long salt and pepper
hair framed his face, a matted,
mangy looking coat of untamed fur
as found on a beast, not on a person.
He dropped to the curb like a
soiled rag falling from a mechanic's
grease-stained pocket.
A guttural sound escaped his lips
punctuating a physical and personal pain.
His eyes lacked the glint that lets you know
there is a spirit within, a zest for contact,
conversation, momentary validation.
I walked past him and felt his eyes
following me, climbing up my back.
Might they be pleading for me to stop?
Might I be the one to bring him
a moment of joy, recognition of being?
Might I be his Good Samaritan?
Then again, as before,
with insecurities bubbling inside,
I kept on walking. Then again,
the words did not come,
I did not look back.

This Church

I see this church as being out in the country, a bit back from the road, and by itself; no accompanying buildings or sheds. Sitting on top of its steeple stands a weathered cross, both needing a paint job. The front doors are open and slightly askew, as if being placed that way from strong winds and neglect over time. There is no sign to indicate a denomination, no visible driveway to usher me in closer.

I walk through waist high weeds and thick grass which entwine my legs, snaring my feet, tripping me, trying to enforce that I am not to go any closer. With some effort, I continue. I feel the beat of my heart increasing in pace as my mind begins to fill with thoughts, questions.

I wonder when the church was built and by whom. Perhaps a corner stone will provide some answers. I do not find one. The front steps are wide, cut from sandstone. They are worn down in the middle from years of wear. How many people walked up and down them? The doors have regular knobs, dull and tarnished; no locks! Everyone had free access. I cross the worn threshold and enter. The air is not clean; it smells musty from abandonment and of the fall of the year. The windows are clear glass and stark, needing color I think. I rub the grime away with my elbow and notice they are wavy, objects on the outside are distorted, really old glass, crafted differently from today.

The plain wooden pews are no longer set in aligned rows. They too show wear from people and the elements, dust catchers for a long time. Exposed rafters above me hold several nests; some look to be old, some new, though no birds chirp warnings or buzz the intruder. I see no organ or piano but a simple pulpit front and center on a square platform. How many ministers preached from its pulpit? How many couples said their marriage vows here, infants baptized, communions administered?

I step up to stand behind the pulpit and imagine full pews with attentive listeners both adult and child. How many people attended services here, witnessed funeral memorials? How many hymns sung here? I close my eyes and hear the music; I open them to see smiling faces, joyful expressions, singing with passion, not a hymnal in sight. "Rock of ages, cleft for me, Let me hide myself in Thee...." I wonder how much joy and sorrow seasoned these walls? "Twas grace that taught my heart to fear, And grace my fears relieved...."

I choke back emotion, retreat to the doors and beyond. I return to the graveled road and look back at the church. It's gone! No church, just a field full of waist high weeds and thick grass. But the church was there! I was in it! What kind of trick of the imagination is being played? I remember asking my grandpa if the church was familiar to him. He said no, as did my mother in response to the question. Yet I see this church often, when I close my eyes and at night when I dream.

Why does this church haunt me so? Could it be an earlier life thing?

The Time is Now

It is inevitable!
You cannot be serious!
Better now than never.
Why?
Because.
Here?
Yes!
You're nuts!
Maybe so.
Too soon!
Now seems right.
Not so!
Why not?
Not yet!
Okay.
Are you kidding?
Are you?
I hate that grin!
What grin?
That ornery one!
Then forget it.
Do you mean it?
Yes.
Really?
No.
I thought so!
Well then…
Well then what?
You know….

Time Was...

People viewed work and play
as having different rules.

Chalk art on sidewalks
buffered the angry footsteps of hate.

School playgrounds and cafeterias
were places of laughter and nourishment
rather than death scenes.

People embraced one another
without derogatory interpretations.

People spoke in eloquent language
and were curious about
the world and their place in it.

Adults would comfort a crying child
rather than walk on by.

People understood
they owed the world a living,
not the reverse.

Peaches and cream
was a luscious treat
not viewed as fat, fiber or calories.

People developed governments
so governments could protect people.

People rarely locked their houses and left the
keys in the ignitions of their cars, rather than
invest in home and auto security devices.

Time was...
you didn't worry about tomorrow,
you knew it would be better.

Tracks

The clumps of tall brown grass
provided a wind break for
the animal that rested at the base
allowing soft snow to pile up
around its warm blooded form.
I could see its tracks easing out
into the fresh snow, timid tracks
grouped in close fashion, two or three
short hops followed by indentations
from its resting body weight.
The tracks continued for another
ten yards then abruptly lengthened
into the long strides that
reflected it was on the move.
Zigging and zagging, the tracks
revealed the hectic attempt to
flee, a desperate flight for safety,
a rabbit on the run.
The tracks ended at a gouge.
Tufts of fur and blood,
tainting the purity of the snow,
documented the killing field.
The hunter's tracks approached
the kill then diverged to
a ninety degree angle,
in pursuit of another thrill.

While looking at the scene,
I recalled killing my first rabbit,
remembered reveling in my success
congratulated by my brother
with a hug and whoops of joy.
I continued hunting into my college years
motivated by the thrill of the hunt,
time spent bonding with my buddies,
and a love for mom's fried wild rabbit
with pan gravy and mashed potatoes.
But on this day, now in my late twenties,
there was no thrill to these tracks,
no desire to follow in the footsteps
of the hunter.

Ubiquitous

I feel its presence, its being
everywhere at the same time,
constantly encountering me
not matter where I am or go.
I get this all-over and
ever-present notion that
it somehow extends from me
while at the same time
hides from me.
Shy, it appears only at night
in my house on the walls
or in the sunlight of day;
it documents my presence,
does my shadow.

Ultimate

"Dad, there are a lot of words that are pretty confusing."

"I know, son, there are lots and lots of words that are hard to figure out."

"Take the word, fair. I just don't think I understand it, Dad. Everyone seems to have their own meaning for it. What seems fair to one person never seems fair to another person. How could it mean so many different things?" He shook his head side to side in confusion. "What does it mean to you?"

"Well, son, to me it means playing by the rules, being honest, not trying to take advantage of anyone, trying to do things the right way so that no one gets hurt. That's what fair means to me. Fair means trying to treat each other with honesty. I think it is the ultimate respect given to a person."

"Boy, that doesn't sound like an easy thing to do! What does ultimate mean?"

"First, being fair is not easy to be. You have to be willing to be flexible in your way of thinking. Being fair is often situational; what might be fair in one, may not be fair in another. When people are kind to each other, then it is much easier to be fair. Second, ultimate means it can not get better; it is a part of a person's goodness."

"It's almost like the Golden Rule, isn't it? You know, treating others as you would like to be treated. The Golden Rule is a kind of ultimate isn't it?"

"Pretty much so. People judge you, in part, on how fair they think you are. Unfortunately, no matter how fair you try to be, there is always somebody who will think you are not fair. Even when you think you have done your very best, some people will think you could have done better."

"I guess that's one of those adult things, huh Dad?"

"No, it's the ultimate, it's one of those people things!"

Unknown

One side of the brain understands
there is much to be positive about;
the other side of the brain
struggles with such a notion,
rebels against all things positive,
at odds with the idea.
When the brain cannot reach consensus,
is there no wonder the body behaves
out of sorts and idiosyncratic?
There is an outcry here,
a scream of anguish so deep inside
we may never find the source of unreason.
We are left with the chaos, horror,
misery the behavior produces.
We want to find an answer,
demand one, because
we are unsettled with the unknown.
Life's preparation requires years of learning,
of finding solutions to the unknown.
The concept of the unknown
makes us feel incomplete,
as if we have failed in some way
with our preparation.
We exclaim with anger and frustration,
"I'll never understand!"
The exclamation, however,
doesn't appease our unrest
or distaste; tears and hugs,
while momentarily comforting,
will not erase the happening of the event.
Too often, for too long,
we continue to ponder
to search for the answer.
When the answer is not forthcoming,
we often lose faith and give up hope.
The appalling act claims another victim.
Perhaps some unknowns
are better left not known.
To accept that is to move on.

Usages

I wish I had a dollar for every time I was told to use a dictionary to locate meanings of words I wanted to employ. For many years I accepted such direction as the appropriate process used to locate meaning. Then I discovered that was not the case; dictionaries are primarily employed to verify spellings and identify the usages of words. Some words have few usages, other words have many. Dictionaries list such usages for the reader. Meanings, on the other hand, are personal interpretations of a given usage of any word, when placed by its context.

Meanings are in people. Word usages are found in dictionaries.

Useless

Samantha set her jaw. She hated feeling the way she did now, that emptiness inside, the one that screams to be let out. When it gets out, it jumps on your face, jabs at your chest, and slices your heart out by hurling the word useless at you through clenched teeth.

For as long as she could remember, others had called her weak, inept, worthless, inefficient, and hopeless. They forced womanhood onto her whether she wanted it or not. When she couldn't do womanly things right, the way others expected, she was ridiculed, made fun of.

She enjoyed working on cars, tearing engines apart and repairing them, to hear them purr like a kitten. She loved camping out, hiking, rappelling cliffs, and exploring. She felt fulfilled when she rode motorcycles on cross-country excursions.

She did not enjoy wearing makeup, doing her hair everyday, wearing skirts, cleaning house, ironing, mending, or cooking. When she got hungry, she went to a drive-thru, or called for pizza. She did believe in clean clothes and did her own laundry. Why not?

She was also lonely. She longed for something she did not have: a girlfriend. Guys were great, but some things should not be shared with a guy. Once shared, guys have a tendency to cast you aside like a used paper plate.

Every time she met a woman she thought would become a good friend the relationship would flounder and she would be thrown into the useless pile for one with more domestic skills, who was more fashionable, had more in common. Each time a futility set in. She would feel useless.

Verbs

Commonly considered as action words;
to express acts or occurrences.

Like all children, I epitomized
the verb on a daily basis.
I vaulted over everything I could because
up and over seemed quicker than around.
I was told I vocalized too much
and was rarely on pitch.
I ejected from the barn beams and
into the haystack below because
of the chills that ran down my spine.
I embraced my aunties and held on for dear life
when their laughter threatened to throw me off.
I rustled cows and corralled rustlers with my playmates.
My mother let me stir the batter
and my grandmother let me beat the rugs.
I loved bouncing on the hay wagons in the bumpy fields
and sliding from side to side in the back
of the Jeep on curvy dirt roads.
I was scolded often.
I had to scrub my skin clean more than my liking.
I enjoyed slurping my drinks too loudly
and sprawling all over the place when sitting.

I must admit that I loved being a kid.
I think verbs exist to describe
the traits and actions of childhood.
Don't you?
When we are adults, and we
allow the child within to escape,
we drag verbs along for good measure.

"Without knowing the force of words, it is impossible to know more."
—Confucius

Vertigo

VERSE that is
ESCALATING
RADIATING
TRANSCENDING
INDULGING
GROPING
OVERSTIMULATING

often disorders us.

Watering Hole

I did not sleep well and quietly edged out
of the tent into early morning light.
Antiseptic air entered my lungs
to kick-start my body's energy plant.

Wet flora slapped my bare legs as I
navigated my way to the bend in the creek.
Erosive spring thaws from the high hills
made this place a perfect watering hole.

I froze in my footsteps just
as she turned to look at me.
Her black bandit mask and beady eyes
locked in on my presence.

Sniffing the air for my scent
she cautiously put her body between me
and her two babies, a safety barrier
they eagerly tried to glimpse around.

Sensing no danger, she continued her
task of morning facials,
reminding me of my mother's
insistence upon clean faces before breakfast.

She nudged them away from the water's edge.
Her senses more acute than mine,
she picked up the doe and yearling
approaching to my right.

Hypnotized, I could barely draw breath at the
beauty of this magic moment.
Moving nothing but my eyes,
I dined on this dessert of nature's buffet.

Is there a look gentler than that in a deer's eyes?
Parenting more caring than that of a mother raccoon?

When All is Said and Done

What is left at the end of a long, hard day
when all has been said and done?

Some would say nothing is left.
Some will say cold, hunger, and emptiness.
Some would say hope for a better day.
Others would profess accomplishment and success.
Others proclaim love and passion.
Still others may say peace.

Most nights, my muscles ache as I
lower by body onto bed.
My mind is weary and not always clear.
But I thank God for the day,
every one a gift.
When all is said and done,
at my age, a day
to learn from, enjoy, and
be thankful for.

Why

Why is it that when people
are confronted with something
negative in their life they always exclaim,
"Why is this happening to me?"

Why is it that when people
face happy, joyous, positive occasions
so few of them utter,
"Why is this happening to me?"

"Why don't I do the right thing
when it needs to be done?"
"Why are you doing this to me?"
"Why do you make a joke out
of everything? Get serious!"

"Why are people nasty to each other?"
"Why doesn't God hear my prayers?"
"Why do I have to go to school?"
"Why does Sheila always get her way?"
"Why don't you love me?"

"Why do some people have
inquiring minds, while others
do not?"

Other than the conjunction "and,"
is there another three letter word
used as often as is "why?"

Yes?

Win or Lose

"It is not whether you win or lose,
but how you play the game."
Words to learn and live by,
instilled in youngsters, like myself,
in days gone by from caring adults
who understood the reasons why.

Where have the concepts of fair play
and sportsmanship gone?
It was pushed to the wayside by
greed, power, and attitudes
of win at all costs learned today
by children at very early ages;
from adults who lost sight
of the right and honorable way.

Influenced by walks of life, activities
filled with wanton abuse, malicious cheating,
negative campaigning, steroid propagation
serving as prophetic and predictive
opiates for our future generations.
Actions condoned by people who
feel no guilt and openly
justify their deeds under
the guise of unearned entitlements;
accepting the notion
that everybody does it.

I long for days when fair play
and good sportsmanship are
learned and lived rather
than learned then cast aside
when the going gets tough.
Days when honesty reasserts itself
and the processes of decision making
and problem solving are aimed
at win-win models rather than
models of win-lose, or lose-lose.

Winter Creaks

The house announced the seasons
as regular as a town crier heralded
"All is well," days long ago.

He imagined a large pitcher pouring milk
over the roof, eliciting the snap, crackle,
and pop echoing throughout the rooms.

The moaning and groaning timbers
recorded each plunge of the thermometer.
Gusts of wind ripped long cursing creaks
from one end of the house to the other.

If the house could speak in his language,
it would plead to be protected
from winter's freezing fury.

He pulled the blankets tighter under his chin.
Deep orange embers peeked at him through the dark,
begging to be tended before
ebony pitch embraced the night.

Edging from the bed,
knees creaking as he righted himself,
his body spoke, as did the house.

He probed the embers with the poker,
coaching feeble flames.
They fed on tinder and sprightly
danced for the fire master.

Shadows played tag against the walls.
Creaks of winter prodded his memories.
He pulled his head under the blankets;
where he would remain until the break of day.

Wisdom

comes from great suffering,
  so sayeth the golden Greeks.
A product of failure and triumph;
  an awareness that good,
  or bad, can happen.
Discovering "the joy of parenting"
  gets magnified when staring into
  the faces of grandchildren.
Understanding why watching
  a sleeping child caresses
  the heart in a manner
  foreign to any other touch.
Admitting a wrong
  and working to correct it
  is accepting responsibility.
Intelligence is enhanced through
  readings and teachings.
Wisdom is the acquisition
  of learning from experiences.

Within the Sublime

Within the simple, lies the silly.
    Within the silly, lies the sublime.
        Within the sublime, lies a hint of reality.
    Within reality, lies a thread of discomfort.
When discomforted, we raise our guards.

Then we laugh, to keep from imploding.

Words Walk

Words,
vocabulary,
formal and informal,
foreign or domestic,
are the basis for reading,
for speech,
for writing,
for communication
within and between cultures.

We need to understand that words walk.
They take us by the hand and escort us
to places where our minds and
imaginations thrive.

Yap

Over the years,
yap has been used
to describe noisy chatter,
scolding behavior,
crude talk, and
rambling conversation.
I have fallen into the yap trap.
Brevity has not been one
of my conversational traits.
I apologize to all of my victims.
Having said that,
it is time to shut up!

About the Author

Ronald M. Ruble, born in Shelby, Ohio, 1940, is an Associate Professor Emeritus of Humanities at Firelands College of Bowling Green State University, Huron, Ohio. He is the father of two sons, Eric and Kristofer, and has six grandchildren. He is a 1962 graduate of Otterbein University and received his Ph.D. from Bowling Green State University in 1975. He is an award winning playwright (*My Father's Father.*) He has earned national awards as a poet and fiction writer and has published his work in *Grand Lake Review*, *The Heartlands Today*, *Poet's Corner*, and *Verses Magazine*. His writing can also be found in anthologies by Bottom Dog Press, Cader Publishing, Doll Printing Press, Eber & Wein, Iliad Press, Noble House, Quill Books, and Watermark Press. *Words Walk* follows his first book, *The Pulse of Life* (2005). He is presently Poet Laureate of Huron, Ohio.

OTHER BOOKS BY BIRD DOG PUBLISHING

The Wonderful Stupid Man by Allen Frost
978-1-933964-64-5   190 pgs. $15
Dogs and Other Poems by Paul S. Piper
978-1-933-64-45-4   74 pgs. $15
The Mermaid Translations by Allen Frost
978-1-933964-40-9   136 pgs. $15
Home Recordings by Allen Frost
978-1-933964-24-9   124 pgs. $15
Faces and Voices: Tales by Larry Smith
1-933964-04-9   136 pgs. $15
Second Story Woman: A Memoir of Second Chances
by Carole Calladine
978-1-933964-12-6   226 pgs. $16
256 Zones of Gray: Poems by Rob Smith
978-1-933964-16-4   80 pgs. $15
Another Life: Collected Poems by Allen Frost
978-1-933964-10-2   176 pgs. $15
Winter Apples: Poems by Paul S. Piper
978-1-933964-08-9   88 pgs. $15
Lake Effect: Poems by Laura Treacy Bentley
1-933964-05-7   108 pgs. $14
Depression Days on an Appalachian Farm: Poems
by Robert L. Tener
1-933964-03-0   80 pgs. $15
120 Charles Street, The Village: Journals & Other Writings 1949-1950
by Holly Beye
0-933087-99-3   240 pgs. $16

Bird Dog Publishing
A division of Bottom Dog Press, Inc.
PO Box 425/ Huron, Ohio 44839
Order Online at:
http://smithdocs.net/BirdDogy/BirdDogPage.html

Bottom Dog Press

Books in the Harmony Series
Painting Bridges: A Novel
By Patricia Averbach, 234 pgs. $18
Ariadne & Other Poems
By Ingrid Swanberg, 120 pgs. $16
The Search for the Reason Why: New and Selected Poems
By Tom Kryss, 192 pgs. $16
Kenneth Patchen: Rebel Poet in America
By Larry Smith, Revised 2nd Edition, 326 pgs. Cloth $28
Selected Correspondence of Kenneth Patchen,
Edited with introduction by Allen Frost, Paper $18/ Cloth $28
Awash with Roses: Collected Love Poems of Kenneth Patchen
Eds. Laura Smith and Larry Smith
With introduction by Larry Smith, 200 pgs. $16

* * * *

Harmony Collections and Anthologies
d.a.levy and the mimeograph revolution
Eds. Ingrid Swanberg and Larry Smith, 276 pgs. $20
Come Together: Imagine Peace
Eds. Ann Smith, Larry Smith, Philip Metres, 204 pgs. $16
Evensong: Contemporary American Poets on Spirituality
Eds. Gerry LaFemina and Chad Prevost, 240 pgs. $16
America Zen: A Gathering of Poets
Eds. Ray McNiece and Larry Smith, 224 pgs. $16
Family Matters: Poems of Our Families
Eds. Ann Smith and Larry Smith, 232 pgs. $16

Bottom Dog Press, Inc.
PO Box 425/ Huron, Ohio 44839
Order Online at:
http://smithdocs.net/BirdDogy/BirdDogPage.html

Recent Books by Bottom Dog Press

Sky Under the Roof: Poems By Hilda Downer, 126 pgs. $16.
Breathing the West: Great Basin Poems
By Liane Ellison Norman, 80 pgs. $16
Smoke: Poems By Jeanne Bryner, 96 pgs. $16
Maggot : A Novel By Robert Flanaga, 262 pgs. $18
Broken Collar: A Novel By Ron Mitchell, 234 pgs. $18
American Poet: A Novel By Jeff Vande Zande, 200 pgs. $18
The Pattern Maker's Daughter: Poems
By Sandee Gertz Umbach, 90 pages $16
The Way-Back Room: Memoir of a Detroit Childhood
By Mary Minock, 216 pgs. $18
The Free Farm: A Novel By Larry Smith, 306 pgs. $18
Sinners of Sanction County: Stories
By Charles Dodd White, 160 pgs. $17
Learning How: Stories, Yarns & Tales
By Richard Hague, 216 pgs. $18
Strangers in America: A Novel
By Erika Meyers, 140 pgs. $16
Riders on the Storm: A Novel
By Susan Streeter Carpenter, 404 pgs. $18
The Long River Home: A Novel
By Larry Smith, 230 pgs. Paper $16/ Cloth $22
Landscape with Fragmented Figures: A Novel
By Jeff Vande Zande, 232 pgs. $16
The Big Book of Daniel: Collected Poems
By Daniel Thompson, 340 pgs. Paper $18/ Cloth $22;
Reply to an Eviction Notice: Poems
By Robert Flanagan, 100 pgs. $15
An Unmistakable Shade of Red & The Obama Chronicles
By Mary E. Weems, 80 pgs. $15
Our Way of Life: Poems By Ray McNiece, 128 pgs. $15

Bottom Dog Press, Inc.
PO Box 425/ Huron, Ohio 44839
Order Online at:
http://smithdocs.net/BirdDogy/BirdDogPage.html